LIVING THROUGH THE DARKNESS
A FIREFIGHTER/PARAMEDIC'S STORY OF
OVERCOMING LIFE'S TRAGEDIES

MELISSA A. PARKER

Title: Living Through The Darkness. A firefighter/paramedic's story of overcoming life's tragedies.

ISBN: 9780578584478

Subjects: Motivation | Self Help | Psychology

Cover Design by Melissa Parker

Printed In the United States of America

To those who supported me through my growth, and
those who continue to help guide me today.

An even special thank you to the therapists and
clinicians who educated me on how to be the best me,
for myself and for anyone I encounter.

<u>About The Book</u>

So, look... I'm not here to write a book to coddle you in, make you feel fluffy and warm, or make you feel happier about yourself. This is all on you. What I am here to do is give you some insight on how to work toward your goal of being a happy fucking person again, because you and I both know that being miserable sucks.

I am not a mental health professional. I am just a little transplant firefighter/paramedic from Maine that moved to Kentucky to live a more fulfilling career as such, not realizing that I would fall victim to the mental illness that has plagued our profession. In being a glorious victim (*enter sarcasm here*), I felt that my story and journey would share its relevance to your life or some aspect of it. Hopefully by doing such, this can help motivate you to take some steps toward being a happy fucking person. You're not alone, even if you think you are. I can promise you that.

I'm not going to censor anything here, so if you get easily hurt or triggered, this book may not be for you. I am going to tell things like they are, the way I have seen them, or experienced them. I am sharing pieces of my life, for which you can combine into my later life experiences, in hopes for you to understand your own life better. I am not sugar-coating shit. No fluff here. I am a sister out here trying to scream it to the top of the world that you're not alone and that there is help for you.

I have been through shit. I have been abused, bullied, lied to, cheated on, homeless, and everything in between. I've drank, done drugs, been to jail, and always made everyone else my priority, all while looking down on myself no matter what achievements I got in life or hurdles I was able to jump over.

This is my story.

1

Childhood

I was born in Brunswick Maine in 1982. I was 7lbs 12oz, and a bundle of joy. My parents had planned to have me, and to my father, a baby girl was exactly what he wanted. He was thrilled to have a little baby girl. A girl whose birthdays would be full of summer adventures. My brother would finally have the little sister to protect growing up and it was perfect timing.

I don't remember much of my childhood, but from pictures it looked like I lived a wonderful one. I saw pictures of my father and I swimming, and pictures of my mother giving me a perm by the kitchen sink. It was crazy how I looked with rollers in my hair, but in all those pictures I was happy. As I aged more into my adolescent years, I could see some changes. Pictures were not as common, or happy for that matter, and I can remember some of those times. Times that I didn't realize, would affect me well into my adulthood.

I played a lot of sports, and attendance by my parents were hit and miss. Soccer games were usually around 4 or sometimes later, and my mother would make them when she could. My dad never did come to any of my soccer games in high school from what I can recall. He attended a few while I was in middle school. Softball games my father attended from time to time, but of course my mother was in attendance the most.

My mother worked for the United States Navy as a management analyst for the OIG (Officer of the Inspector General), and my father was in the US Navy for a four-year term and left. He later became disabled and was unable to work. Mom was the supplier and wore the pants in the family. She worked, cooked, cleaned, and did her best to spend time with me once dad became disabled. She mowed the lawn, would fix electrical and plumbing problems in the house, and even built the steps leading into the basement from outside.

The story about my father is a rather lengthy one, but I don't want to spend this entire book focusing on my family. There are reasons why this is included, and you will hopefully understand later in the book. The fact of the matter is, that I will explain the relevant details of my father in this chapter, and you can do the mind work as you continue to read along. Sound good? Great, let's go!

My father was in the Navy, and stationed aboard the USS Edward McDonnell (FF-1043), a frigate, out of New England. My mother met him during his service time, and of course you know what happened after that. He was up for promotion and was set on making the US Navy a 20-year career. His fellow shipmates and officers encouraged him to apply for promotion. Long story short, he was not given the promotion. Despite an almost 4 year, record free and honorary service term, he was denied promotion and it shattered his motivation to stay in the service.

He wrote a long and professional letter to the division chief, explaining that his commitment to the US Navy was something he took pride in and he wanted to make it his life, but since being denied a promotion after almost 4 years of extraordinary service, he was not going to reenlist. I was able to find all this out after my mother died in January of 2019.

My father finished his contract in 1981 and did not reenlist in the US Navy. Now, being as I was born in 1982, he had picked up a job in central Maine at a manufacturing facility of Nerf equipment. Sometime several years later, he had an exposure illness that ultimately led him to disability, and he was unable to work due to different types of treatments he had to get a result of such.

He had been a beer drinker for as long as I remember, but I do remember not too long after he became disabled, he started drinking Vodka and tonic quite frequently. He was an avid billiards player, a good one at that, and was part of a members only bar. He spent a lot of time there and would often come home intoxicated. Yes, he was driving. I remember the first, and only time, that he was involved in an automobile accident. He was driving on River Road in Lewiston

Maine, leaving the bar he was a member of, when his vehicle lost control and he flipped it multiple times, landing him along the bank of the Androscoggin River. His vehicle was totaled, and he was one flip away from going into that river. Of course, he survived, without a scratch, but that incident lead my mother to tell him to go to rehab, or get divorced.

My father went to rehab, and was successful, for a short period of time anyway. I laugh as I think about it just because as a kid I really didn't understand what was going on, but by the time he got back to drinking again, it was all hands-on deck for me, with a heightened sense of awareness, and a constant state of fear. His concoction of vodka and tonic had turned into straight vodka. No chaser, no middleman, just the hard, nasty, clear Five O'clock Vodka. I would find a bottle from time to time and open it up enough to smell it. It amazed me how someone could drink it, as awful as it smelled. Even to this day, when I visit back home, and happen to see one sitting on the shelf at the liquor store, I don't understand how anyone can buy and drink that shit, and it always brings back memories of my father.

Mom would get up around 5am, Monday through Friday, and get ready for work at the Brunswick Naval

Air Station. She had a very important job. She would occasionally have to go to the Naval Base in Rhode Island for audits, and did some travelling with her job, but that meant that I was with dad most of the daytime hours. Mom would get home between 4pm and 5pm. Of course, I had school, unless it was a vacation day or school break, and I would be gone till school let out around 2:15pm.

This brings me back to a quick note. I was in and out of trouble in middle school. I got bullied by a couple of people from time to time, mostly because of how short and skinny I was. I was tied to a tree by my next door neighbor's kids using seatbelts, in the middle of winter, and my gloves and knit hat were buried in the snow. I was shot with a BB gun by a kid that lived down the street. I was chased and pushed off my bike by another guy that lived down the street, who today is serving a life sentence in prison for murder.

Even some of the teachers at my middle school were very condescending toward students. My grades were acceptable, and yet I was blocked from attending homecoming. They never gave my mother or I a reason a to why, but I showed up dressed up, and was told I was not allowed to attend. I was later expelled in middle school for leaning across the table in class while my feet stayed on the floor. Yes, expelled. My mother decided to home school me for the rest of my middle school years, and I only engaged in summer sports. The principle was eventually fired for locking a student in a closet.

By the time I was to return to high school, my mother allowed me to go back, just so that I could play sports. Sports were my life, and I did everything I could to maintain my grades, just so that I could continue to play. It was my escape from home, and motivation to do something good and something healthy.

I had an array of friends. I was friends with the sporty, intelligent students, and I was friends with the pot smokers and trouble makers. I hung out with the sporty friends during school hours, and when I was out of school, I hung out with the trouble makers. I liked being friends with everyone. I didn't want to be one of the people that was a member of a "click". I just wanted to be a cool kid! And I was, so I thought.

I started to come home to a progressively more intoxicated father. He would immediately start out certain conversations with a hostile tone of voice.

"Where the fuck have you been?"

It was always common sense that when I came home, my intentions were to go to my room, and work on homework. Well, that didn't happen much. The distractions were so high because he would constantly be bitching about something, whether it made sense or not, and he would be looking for a verbal confrontation. If I ignored him, he would make sure he voiced that as well. Things would only escalate from there.

"How's my little boy been doing? What trouble did you cause today?"

He always had some snide remark to say to me when he was drunk. He would go on and on with some sort of blabber bullshit until he was blue in the face, or until you acknowledged his conversation. I would ignore him and shut the door. He would come into the hallway, as I leaned against the door to keep him from coming in. He would smack the door with his palm.

"You listening to me you little bitch?"

I would still manage not to say a word, until he had hit the door so hard in anger, that he would put a hole in it. This went on over quite some time. There were holes in several of the doors, and eventually a larger one in the wall, from the back of my head. Dad's verbal abuse went on for a couple of years, as his drinking became heavier and heavier, until it finally got to the point of the physical abuse.

Going home then ended up with dishes and chairs being thrown at me as I would rush into my bedroom. I knew the door would protect me, because I was strong, and I was strong enough to keep him from getting in. I took several years of Shaolin Kempo, and my father would taunt me saying,

"Why don't you use your karate to hit me? Go ahead".

I never wanted to strike my father. I knew if I truly let out my anger on him, that I would risk killing him, and that was just something I didn't need in my life, especially with my criminal background. I never used my crime as an excuse for my behavior, but as time brings me here today, I understand more about why I went that route.

I was in and out of the Androscoggin County Jail, and the Maine Youth Center, since I was 13 years old. Everything from criminal threatening, to forgery, theft, and assault. I got so bad that my mother couldn't even handle dealing with my behavior and my father's behavior in the summer time, so I was sent to a group home for the summer months in Lewiston Maine, with other troubled teenagers. There, I began to smoke cigarettes, marijuana, and meet other people that did the same. It got so bad, I was kicked out of there too, and it was part of my probation to behave. My mother didn't know what to do, and home life was getting worse.

The final straw with my father was late spring of 1997. I came home to an outraged man. I had found one of his vodka bottles, and emptied it, filling it with water. He went crazy. He was chasing me around the kitchen island, throwing anything he could at me. I was dodging cups, flyswatters, and anything else he could get his hands on. I ran down the hallway and he caught me just before I passed the bathroom. He pushed me against the wall, causing me to slam my head into the wall putting a hole in it. His hands were going around my throat, as I broke out and escaped out the front door. I ran as fast as I could to my best friend's house on the opposite corner, crying. They knew how my father was. I didn't have to tell much of a story, as this was becoming routine.

The police had been to the house, but because of my criminal history, the police didn't do anything. The police never believed me no matter what I complained about. They didn't believe me even when I was innocent. I was always to blame. I stole from mom so much that when money went missing at a time that I didn't take any, she would instantly blame me, and never believe me when I said I didn't. It got so bad that my friends' parents didn't want me hanging out with their kids anymore, and of course that spread to the police. I was nothing but trouble.

My friend and I watched out the back porch as my mother pulled into the driveway. I knew it would be safe to go home when she arrived. You see, dad never hit me in front of mom, and dad seldom called me the horrible things he had, in front of her. When I returned home, it was a whole other story. My mother saw the hole in the wall and confronted my father about it. Of course, he started cussing at her and blaming my behavior for it. I then told mom he tried to strangle me and that I went to my friend's house. That sealed the deal. Mom told dad to get out of the house, and that was that.

Dad moved above the members only bar he went to. There was an apartment above it where another friend of his lived. Mom filed for a divorce, and my father didn't argue with it. It was a clean-cut divorce. He had nothing she needed, and he didn't go after her for the house or anything else. His alcoholism and violent behavior let me see him on weekends if I wanted to, only if he was sober. He was sober when my visits were arranged, but I did notice something about him that was not normal. My father was always thin. He was a thin, fit looking man, who was pale and freckled with red hair. He was your typical Irishman. Well, he had gained an astronomical amount of weight. His arms, legs, and belly were all swollen. I asked him what was wrong, and he just explained that he was retaining water, but that he was fine. That was the last time I spoke to my father.

My father had fallen down the stairs of the apartment he shared, on the first of September. He was taken to Central Maine Medical, where he was in a coma. Diagnosis: Multiple Liver Cirrhosis. He was unplugged from the ventilator on the 3rd, then cremated and buried with his father in his hometown in Massachusetts. I was 15 years old, and I didn't feel that upset at the time of his death, but later in life, I wished he could see where I was now.

What ultimately lead me to a sentence until my 18th birthday was my mother telling the judge to put me away. I was so out of control, that in September of 1999, I was being tried for forgery of my mothers' checks. She couldn't handle me anymore. She had so much stress on her, that she mentally could not handle me. I ended up with a sentence to the Maine Youth Center. I was 17. My mother would visit me on the weekends, and I would find out that any chance of me playing college soccer or softball was over because of my jail time. It was a hard hit for me. I was in a correctional facility with murderers, sexual offenders, and other severe crimes. I never killed anyone or even cut anyone. I got in one fight that landed me with an assault charge, but because I was on probation for that, the forging of my mother's check was the last straw. I felt like I didn't belong in there. Like my crimes were in no comparison to others. Sadly, I paid to play the game. I thought I was such a badass on the streets, that now I was a weak link in the system. For those long months, I sat in a single room cell, and there too, I was segregated.

The months went by and by. A close high school teacher became a mentor, just so she could come and see me. She gave me words of encouragement and filled my heart with self-love and acceptance. I was so motivated by her positive words, that I vowed to get out and change my life. Most other teachers and parents said I would never go anywhere in life. I would go back to jail, never get a job, and end up a bum. I didn't want that. I wasn't going to let that happen. I was truly blessed to have such a wonderful teacher that believed in me. I am still friends with her to this day.

My lifestyle lead me to be isolated in a single room versus being in a women's dorm room. Even though my intentions there were not to make friends, or girlfriends for that matter, the fact that I chose an alternative lifestyle made certain staff members uncomfortable, and I was not allowed to be in a dorm area at night.

I was a very talented artist, and I received a sketch book of the human figure to draw from. It was removed because it had sketches in it that consisted of naked men and women. I was doing everything I could to get the fuck out of there.

I walked out of those gates the day before my 18th birthday. I looked back, gave the place the middle finger and a "fuck you", and said "hello" to a new world ahead of me.

"Get ready, because I am going to do great things."

My father and I during the good years.

2

Starting Over

Mom paid for me to take some college classes. I signed up at Central Maine Community College and took College Writing, and the Emergency Medical Technician course. I was pretty set on becoming an Emergency Medical Technician and a Firefighter. My childhood friends' father, and youth summer softball coach, was to blame for that. He was a career fireman, and I looked up to him a lot. Not to mention he played kind of my fathers' role after my father died.

I passed college writing with flying colors but I did always have a knack for writing. I had a few pieces of poetry published as a kid, and as I got older, I had a few articles published in newspapers and such. I failed my first EMT class. I didn't put forth the effort enough and I knew in order to pass I needed to study. I mean, this was someone's life that I would eventually be trying to save right? So, I worked a fulltime job till I could save up enough money and I took the class again. I indulged myself in my studying and found it to be more interesting than I intended. After 4 months of constant studying, I finally passed the class. I took the National Registry in 2002 and was finally a certified Emergency Medical Technician.

I picked up a part-time job at a fire department along the coast and volunteered in the mountainous region. In the meantime, as a source of income, I traveled across the country as a successful disc jockey. I'm not talking wedding parties. I was DJing raves. Electronic music, Technics turntables, and vinyl records were my weakness. I had dabbled with the DJing since I was young but got caught up with some new friends who kind of got me headed in the direction of live shows. Before I knew it, I was being booked at some of the biggest and best events across the nation, and in some of the biggest cities. I was getting $600-$700 a night for one hour of headline time, all travel, food, and lodging covered, free bar tab, and free drugs. It was a rockstar lifestyle and I was falling in love with it.

Guys at the fire department knew about my DJing and would ask about the wonderful benefits I would get from it. I enjoyed sharing my experiences with it. I stayed single most of the time, leaving my options just for party goers. It was a smooth life, but some people were skeptical of my new full-time job that kept me out of state two to three times a week. When I finally started traveling out of the country, people got even more concerned, as some of the places I went to were dangerous. Very dangerous. My involvement with drugs was not really a frequent thing, but I knew my coworkers thought about it.

My mother suggested I wasn't really going anywhere. Finding a full-time job was hard for me because of the lack of experience being twenty-two, and the fact that I still had friends that were not productive in life either. She suggested that I start over somewhere besides the little town of Lisbon Falls, that I grew up in. I had met someone named Sam at a rave that I played in Pittsburg, who was an investor, and who I had befriended over the last few months. We talked frequently, and before I knew it, we had developed more than a friendship.

I flew to Kentucky to visit Sam. I stayed for a week or so and explored the marvelous state. We saw some cool places. It was just like Maine but without an ocean. I liked it so much that I considered moving there. The thought was difficult because it was hard leaving a state that I grew up in. With all the negative shit that I had done in my life and the negative people I was around, I needed to start over. I went back home to Maine, pondered on it for a couple months, and decided to pack my shit and move to Kentucky with Sam.

We lived in Frankfort for about a year, before the DJing got to my head, and I ended up breaking up over the phone, and immediately sleeping with someone else. I moved out and started going to college full-time to obtain my associates degree in Fire-Science. I worked a full-time job doing something besides EMS during the two years I was in college, and when I completed college, I got back into fire and EMS. My life began to change in good, and bad ways. I was heavier into drugs, promiscuity, and drinking. I thoroughly enjoyed cocaine and speed, and it got to the point that I was including it in my contracts to play in certain places. Miami, Indianapolis, New York City, Chicago, Detroit, Philadelphia, Sacramento; they all welcomed me with a concoction of substances and liquor. I enjoyed being full of energy, and a party pleaser.

Drinking was beginning to become a problem as well. Though I wouldn't drink while working, the moment I would get home, I would begin to drink. If I was off on the weekend, I spent it all drinking. Drugs, alcohol, one-night stands, all while home and travelling alike, it was in my agenda. I didn't know what I was running from, or why I was doing it. I just thoroughly enjoyed it, and I enjoyed the experiences I had during all of it. I however knew that deep down inside, I wanted to focus on my life, and getting my career settled, and find me one person who I could spend my life with. The only problem was that I never thought I was good enough to keep one person happy, or responsible enough to stay at one job for 20 years.

DJing at Shawnee Cave in Illinois in 2008

Years went by, and the same things would be happening. New cities, new people, new parties, more drugs, more alcohol, and a residency as a DJ at a bar in Louisville. I made quite a few friends in Louisville, all of whom were truly wonderful people, but people who were kind of like me. It was later that one of my best friends was found dead in a gas station bathroom in Indiana from a heroin overdose. That was when I looked in the mirror and realized that if I kept on my tract of drugs and drinking, that person would eventually be me. That was not what I wanted, so I had to make a change. That change would be everything that I thought I needed.

I quit drinking as much, and only did it on social occasions, and responsibly. Drugs were no longer a factor. I hadn't laid my hands on cocaine, speed, MDMA, mushrooms, or marijuana, in quite some time. The only thing that sucked was because of my use, I couldn't get hired on certain fire departments that I applied for. Why? Well, because my drug use was within the last 3-5 years, and they simply didn't want that. No matter what my certifications were, or how I had changed. It was a no go for the big cities. I felt a bit of disappointment each time I would apply and test for a career fire department, only to be told that someone else was accepted, and the usual "Thank you for applying," each time gave me the feeling of disappointment and sadness. I felt like I pushed so hard to get what I wanted, only to be held back.

I decided that I needed to get my paramedic license. I knew that paramedics were hard to come by, and I figured my experience would lead me to be a good paramedic for any department. That would give me more time to be off drugs, and work toward my goals. I was accepted to a local fire department, where I worked part-time, as a new paramedic student. I passed the interview and began on a Monday. I still held a full-time job working at an EMS service during that time, and pretty much doing paramedic school full-time as well between classroom and clinical hours.

I managed to land, what I thought, was a decent relationship. It went on for a couple of years, until it became controlling because I was gone for so long between work and school. It got so bad my partner didn't believe that I was at work or school and would drive to see if my vehicle was there and go so far as to get into the vehicle and comment about my clothes being in there that I had to change into between class and work. Long story short, my partner got on drugs, tried to attack me with a knife, and I had an EPO placed. It has been several years since then, and I have not had any contact.

I got my paramedic license. It was much easier for me than when I obtained my initial EMT license. It was a nice addition to my state firefighter two certification. I was as ready as I ever would be to hit the streets. I wanted to get some experience as a medic on the streets before I applied to a department that I wanted to call my home. I got on my local volunteer fire department and got hired full time by the corresponding county ambulance service there. I also worked two other part-time paramedic jobs in two different cities. I was truly broken in as a paramedic. I was the black cloud that clocked in every third day, brought their best to the table, and experienced some of the worst.

As an instructor, I often warn my students of the things they may encounter as a first responder. I don't spare any details, and the reason behind that is because I want to create first responders that can focus on the job and keep their composure. I didn't want new responders to think, "I wasn't told that I would be seeing this shit." The instructors that all taught me were salty old men, who had been in the field since the brick phones, Lifepack 5's, and Plano tackle boxes that their drugs were in. I learned wonderful things from the old days, as well as the latest and greatest in emergency medical care. The same went for the fire service. I learned from old salty men, who started their career in hip boots and long coats. Elephant trunk SCBAs, and bushy moustaches. (There is still nothing better than a majestic bushy fireman stache, in my opinion.)

I was beginning to turn my life around. The next several years would be filled with good calls, bad calls, good relationships, bad relationships, a period of being homeless, (Yes homeless, but that's just too boring to write about. There is nothing exciting in my homeless story, other than good friends offered me to stay with them, and I continued to work, and live at work; literally.) almost dying after a tonsillectomy and being medivac'd out on a vent and blood, suicide of one of my best friends, and death of my mother not too long after I started to write this book. I had many accomplishments, awards, recognitions, made many friends, taught many classes, spoke about many things, and just did a bunch of shit. I got so carried away in staying busy, that I was able to ignore the main reason why I was doing so.

I started my own wood crafting business, a leather helmet restoration business, a podcast, and was being a travelling instructor under my own educational business. I was truly wrapping myself up in doing services for others, and forgetting that I needed services for myself.

We are getting ready to get into the grit and grime of the novel. If I haven't lost you yet with my story, then great. If I have, just give this book to someone else.

Maine - 2003

Chapter 3

Living The Dream, Or Living A Nightmare

Everyone knows, that being on the box (the ambulance) comes with all sorts of shit. You have people who call 911 because they have had tooth pain for two weeks and haven't called the dentist. You have people with chronic pain who are seeking pain medication because they used all their prescription. You also have drunks, heartbroken teenagers, panic attacks, knee pain and paper cuts. True life-threatening emergencies are extremely rare, though every patient may be having their own version of an emergency, and it really takes a toll on all the responders.

We train for weeks, months, and years, to be able to provide emergency care in the event of a life-threatening emergency in hopes that we can save you, or your loved ones lives. Some of us become so burnt out that they are not prepared for when a real emergency comes. They automatically think that all calls are bullshit. I hadn't got to that point yet, but years later I was beginning to feel that way.

I can remember our first save. In fact, I still talk to the patient to this day. I say "our" because it's never about "me". All saves are as a result of everything that the teams have done. I only consider calls as saves when their heart stops, you get it beating again, and they walk out of the hospital. In the case of this woman it was me, a volunteer fireman, my partner, and an EMT student who happened to live across the street from the patient. It was such an in-depth call that I will only hit the highlights rather than tell the entire story as it happened. But each and every story had either a good effect or a bad one.

Knockin' On Heaven's Door

The tones had dropped for a frequent flier who was drunk and asking for an ambulance. We went to this patient quite often and usually once or twice daily. We were the only ambulance in the entire county at the time and we always had to stage for safety before we went on scene. While staging, dispatch advised of a female having chest pain far out in the county. I made the decision to clear the frequent flier call and allow police to transport that patient. We made our way out onto the back-country roads to the chest pain call.

We arrived on scene to find Robin, a female who was in obvious distress. She was stating she was mowing her lawn when she began to have sudden chest pain. She was pale, sweaty, and laying on the ground. We immediately went to her side as she began to vomit. My partner and I knew this was possibly a heart attack. We picked her up and placed her on the stretcher, drying her off, and placing the electrodes on her chest to obtain a 12 lead ECG of her heart. Surely enough she was having what we call a widow maker. A clot had formed in her left anterior descending artery, which is responsible for most of the blood flow to the front of the left ventricle of the heart. This was a serious heart attack affecting an area in the most important part of the heart.

We quickly called for a medivac as we began to start IVs, administer intravenous fluids, nitroglycerin, and aspirin. No sooner than getting her IV established, her cell phone rang. It was "Knockin on Heaven's Door" by Guns N' Roses. The patient looked to the ceiling of the ambulance, tensed up and then immediately went into cardiac arrest. Just like that, her heart stopped. Axle Rose somehow knew it was going to happen before we did and our patient was on her way to the light.

We quickly checked for a pulse which was absent and began chest compressions as we hooked up the defibrillator pads. Once the pads were applied the first shock was given. Chest compressions were resumed and the first round of intravenous drugs were given. The patient's neighbor came over and helped by providing oxygenated ventilations to the patient using a bag valve mask. A rhythm check showed us that the patient was in ventricular fibrillation. The second shock was delivered and wouldn't you know it, Robin sat up and looked around asking what was going on. Her heart rate was thready, fast, and she was breathing. She was switched to an oxygen mask as the fluid was being administered in her veins. We met the helicopter at the local helipad and she was airlifted, a cardiac cath was done, and she was released three days later. I caught up with her during her hospital stay while working my second job to tears in her eyes and in my eyes. We exchanged words, hugs, and have been friends ever since. Though I don't see her often because of my busy schedule, she has forever touched my heart and proved to me that I am best fitted for this career. I told her about her cell phone ringing prior to her cardiac arrest. It was rather comical. The things we think of to keep sane. This was our first true save.

The good calls like this are few and far between. But the emotional support you give to so many people on other calls have true value. They are special in their own way. We all touch someone's heart at some point in the day. Be it an elderly man or an elderly female. A lonely person who has lost their loved one and just needs to cry with someone. A child who looks up to you who's running a fever and you make them smile by giving them a stuffed animal. Those smiles are what keep me going on the job.

Some people say the good calls make up for the bad calls. But when you have a string of them in one night it's hard to think about the good ones. After so many fires where you pull bodies out, wrecks with mangled drivers and passengers, fence planks through windshields into victims, child abuse cases where you want to kill the abuser, suicides, murders, shootings, and assaults, they all start adding to this backpack we all carry. On top of that, there are calls where you pour blood, sweat, and tears into and still can't save them. You carry the guilt of not being able to save them and start doubting yourself. You start asking yourself if you could have done something else and maybe they would still be alive. Your sense of self-worth went from being great to nothing.

We all try to find humor in the horror just to cope with the pain. We put each problem into that backpack and it gets heavier and heavier in time. Not just at work, but in our lives outside of work. Once we learn how to put one problem away in the backpack then it's easier to put them all in there. One of the biggest problems I put in my backpack was in 2012. I hadn't even been a paramedic for an entire year yet.

Robin and I at my department graduation in 2015

The Black Cloud

My partner and I worked a very difficult wreck scene with two patients. The vehicle was over an embankment against a tree on its side, and I climbed the vehicle and crawled into the driver side window just to access the patients. The fire department was beginning to cut the roof of the vehicle off as I was trying to keep the patients conscious. The weather was bad and flying was initially declined due to the weather. Another ambulance was dispatched due to the severity of the patients. We were able to successfully extricate both patients within a wonderful time frame and were able to transport each one to a local hospital for quick stabilization prior to being transported to a trauma one facility.

A medivac accepted one of the patients and I took my initial patient by ground. I had an extra crew member with me, as they were on a vent, several medications being administered, and critical. We arrived at the trauma facility about 45 minutes later, and at the same time the medivac arrived with the second patient. They were placed in beds next to each other. I was already super emotional about the run because I didn't think either of them would survive. We cleaned the truck up, got things back in order, finished the report while at the hospital, and began to head back to base. The ground was wet, there was some melted snow along the sides of the road, and the weather was rather cold. It had rained most of the afternoon making the roads slick and hard to navigate.

My partner and I rolled upon what appeared to be a non-injury collision in a popular center city area. We stopped to check and make sure everyone was ok and were advised they had contacted police about the incident and were just waiting. As we were standing there, we saw an apparatus from that city's emergency service coming around the corner, no lights and sirens, just strolling along at a normal speed. Suddenly, the driver exited the vehicle and ran toward us yelling and asking for a paramedic. We were advised that a pedestrian had been hit. We quickly entered our vehicle and made our way down the road just a block or so, when we saw a body in the middle of the roadway. We parked our truck at an angle to block traffic from coming near us, and I exited the passenger side to run up to the victim only to find that they were obviously deceased.

The driver of the other apparatus asked if the patient was ok, and I voiced the condition of the victim in gross details. The driver walked away.

Now, in the moment I was full of anger, sadness, disbelief, and helplessness. I was angry, wondering how someone could just run someone over and not stop. I was sad because after I got to looking at the ID in the wallet the victim was carrying, I realized they were young and attractive, as well as successful. I was in disbelief that people were so sick as to take pictures while the body lay in the road, even though one of the first things I did was cover it up, and I was helpless because there was nothing that I could do.

It wasn't until local first responders arrived on scene that I realized the vehicle that struck the pedestrian was the firetruck. Forty-thousand pounds over the head of a pedestrian. I got to see it and the driver got to picture it. They pictured it as I painted the picture for them, in a way that I would joke about in order to cope with the emotions that I was feeling. That incident led to weeks of investigations, pulling the scab off my wounds, and making me feel smaller and smaller knowing that the firefighter who accidently struck them, was a fellow firefighter. A firefighter who will forever remember me as the one that gave them the bad news. A firefighter who will never be on the job again. A firefighter who will forever have to battle that incident.

I've seen many fucked up things in my years, but the first year of being a paramedic was an eye opener. It all started with this very day. Only one of the passengers of the initial vehicle accident survived, and it was my patient. They underwent extensive rehabilitation and pulled an amazing recovery. But it was a night full of horrible things, and I would never have thought that the incident that happened on our way back to base that night, would be one of the first few problems that I put in that backpack and locked up. The investigators would question my partner and I, saying that they heard we hit the victim killing them. They would say they didn't know where the wallet went, when it turned out that the coroner had it. They would call me on my personal phone, come to my place of work, and constantly interview my partner and I. It was like we were criminals. The only thing that finally stopped that was when a settlement was reached. I had stressed for so long that I would be sitting on a stand telling my story to a judge but it never made it that far. I had constant nightmares shortly after it happened. I didn't want to eat,

I chain smoked cigarettes and thoughts of suicide ran in my head. I just never tried at that point. I would cry frequently and feel horrible about myself.

Time had passed on, and I was over the event for the most part, so I thought. The only thing I wanted to do was to talk to the firefighter who was held responsible for the accident. I heard through mutual friends that they had resigned on medical disability. This absolutely killed me. Going from living the dream to living a nightmare. I just wanted to find them and give them a hug. I wanted to be there for them.

I was struggling too, but thought that I wasn't struggling like they may have been. I was able to talk about the event freely, and a lot of people didn't even know I was there. Not my people anyway. I had mutual friends on the department that the driver was on, and they knew. I carried around this self-image that I was a horrible person for telling that driver about the victim. No matter how hard I tried, I could never get a hold of the driver.

I knew who it was, but they had shut themselves off from a lot of that day. It took me a long time to do that for myself and accept the fact that I can't keep being hard on myself trying to make something happen that may never happen. That's all I did but it took a toll on me too. I was fucked up from that run and I didn't even realize it at the time.I started becoming hypervigilant when I would come across that intersection, be a passenger in a vehicle, or even while driving. I would begin to see the silhouette of a person in the middle of the road in various places at night, and automatically have a startled reaction thinking that the vehicle I was in, was going to hit a person. It would only be a moment later that I would realize it would be a reflection of an object or a shadow of something. I would usually laugh about it and carry on my way.

The nightmares started reappearing again, except the flattened face in the pavement would be looking at me asking for help. I never thought anything of it, but they would make me wake up in a puddle of sweat. It was becoming harder and harder as time went on to sleep an entire night peacefully.

© Lexington Herald Leader

The Big One

The shift had been a decent shift, with plenty of down time. I was assigned to the ambulance at our central station, and typical first due district. It was very early in the morning, all of us cozy in the bed. Our engine company crew consisted of an officer, jump seat, and engineer. Our ambulance was staffed by me and a probationary fireman. Also, in house was a newly promoted, but highly intelligent and seasoned Battalion Chief. The tones dropped for a structure fire at a location within a one to two-minute drive from our station.

We all jumped out of bed, rushed to our units, and donned our personal protective equipment. (Turnout pants with boots, protective hood, and turnout coat.) We jumped into our units and headed to the address. As I went to silence the alert system on my phone, we were pulling into the area and I just saw a huge ball of fire coming from an apartment complex.

"There are going to be a shit ton of victims."

As we pulled into the area, I saw the picture more clearly. I saw a two story, multi-dwelling complex of modern construction, and the entire roof and second story porch that was on fire. We were immediately in rescue mode as residents from the first floor were exiting and yelling about people that were in the upstairs apartments.

When we are first due, we usually are tasked alongside of the corresponding stations Engine, Truck, or Rescue company. In this case, the Engine company lieutenant advised that we had victims on the C (back side) of the structure and to grab the extension ladder. I quickly donned my self-contained breathing apparatus (SCBA), helmet and gloves, and grabbed the extension ladder, moving it quickly to the C side.

I came around the building from the D (right side) of the structure. As I came around, I could see the silhouette of a person in the second story window on the

BC corner, and I could hear screams for help. I was quickly advised to ladder the window as me and the jump seat fireman began to climb to rescue the victim. The victim had disappeared as the smoke got thick, and then suddenly caught fire, causing the room to flash. We had to abort our attempt to rescue the victim.

We got off the ladder, with a sense of sadness and disappointment, but we knew there were more. I watched as two people come flying out of the second story window of the adjoining apartment, one of them on fire. One yelled that they were ok, and to check on the other one. I quickly grabbed them by their wrists and dragged their body away from the building and up a small hill toward a parking lot where triage was being set up. Their skin coming off on my gloves from their burns.

They advised me they were having difficulty breathing, as the other victim slid up the hill toward us. The burned victim had soot around their mouth and nose suggestive of inhalation burns from the fire. The other person had a broken leg, and told me to prop the burned patient up on their leg so that they could breathe until the other ambulance arrived to the triage area.

When the ambulance arrived, I assisted the crew in getting the patient on the stretcher and into the ambulance. I assisted in getting the airway taken care of and IV access with fluid. The patient was worried about their dogs more than themselves. We did the best we could to keep them calm and stabilize them. Finally, there was a driver to transport them to the ED, where they died shortly after arrival despite our care. The one with the broken leg survived and the dogs made it.

After all was said and done, the structure was a complete loss and deemed intentional. A total of three lives were lost, many other patients, and several displaced. No known working smoke detectors. Most of the people didn't even have a clue.

We went through CISD (critical incident stress debriefing), and this had been the second one in my entire career. None of them have ever been done effectively, and that would explain how so many people become so fucked up over so many fucked up runs. So many fucked up runs that we all think are just part of the job and that they won't bother us later. I'm here to tell you that a proper procedure should be in place to appropriately address the incident, because these will, and do, affect us later.

Aftermath of the fire that claimed the lives of three people and displaced or injured many others.

© The Winchester Sun

There have been several runs that have affected me in my time, from when I first got my paramedic until before I finally reached out for help. The vehicle burning while a boy lay pinned under the dash, half out of the vehicle. His father yelling at my partner and I that we were not doing enough.

"Save him!"

The husband of a woman who was arguing about a TV show, who ended his life in front of her with a .45 hollow point to the head. The multiple hangings we had been on in a row. The children screaming for their dad who chose heroin over them. The elderly man whose throat was slit from ear to ear. The young man who reached up to me to grab my hand, and told me he was going to die, and then died on me. No matter what we did, we couldn't save him. I could go on for days. Most of us could.

You, as the reader, have more than likely experienced shit like this in your time. It's fucked up. Yes. This is shit no one should have to see but we see it. We see it and we put it right into that backpack with all the other ones, thinking that we are coping with it just fine. That backpack is getting full of bad shit. It's time to work on the bad shit. Believe it or not, we can work on the bad shit and make it easier to take out of that backpack and put somewhere else. There is a way to do more than just put a band aid on it.

The worse shit we hold onto and the worse shit we fail to appropriately cope or grieve over, the more those emotions get stored. That little part of your brain that stores those emotions, well, it can only hold onto so much before it becomes overwhelmed. When that happens, we become an emotional wreck, and eventually pop like a balloon. A balloon can only take so much air before it pops. And when this balloon pops it's not a pretty site, and you may never even realize it. The people you love and care about most will feel the wrath of it.

Critical Incident Stress Management

One of the most important, and most neglected tools to help overcome the trauma you endure while on the job, is critical incident stress management. This is the process of mitigating the short or long-term effects that may arise from experiencing a traumatic incident.

Often times agencies tend to offer CISM after an incident but fail to offer preventative measures beforehand. It usually takes one or more people on an agency to be affected by an incident in order to start and learn or implement a true and aggressive mental health program within their agency. Preventative measures, or mental health awareness before incidents, can be useful to individuals who have learned certain ways to cope with their stress as well as outreach options should they feel the need to seek more help.

Just as all firefighters, paramedics, and emergency medical technicians are required to maintain a certain level of continued education annually or biannually, they should also be required to maintain continued education in mental health and addressing the issues that are plaguing our profession. New employees are added to departments all over the country, and mental health awareness should be brought to light during the initial recruit training just as any other firefighter survival tactics or responder wellbeing for health and fitness.

After an incident, affected crew members should participate in a post-incident defusing before going home from shift. This is usually done with everyone involved and incorporates the chaplain and/or peer support team. This will help address any immediate issues following a traumatic event.

Within the first 24-48 hours after a serious traumatic incident, the crews should go through their departments CISM. This is so crew members involved can express their feelings and details of the incident while it is still fresh in their minds, but within a period of time to address any further effects. This should be done by a mental health professional and under the "Mitchell Model" as referenced by the International Critical Incident Stress Foundation. This gives the professional time to determine if continued therapy may be necessary and evaluate the overall mental state of those involved.

Crew members can speak to department chaplains and/or peer support personnel if the department has them in the meantime beforehand. Peer support people should have knowledge of the mental health issues that personnel may face in their career, and be advocates for their departments mental health wellness program. Both of these options should be used until appropriate CISM is done.

Having group support of all those involved is also beneficial. Crews can share their feelings among each other and also look to each other for guidance. It is much easier for members of an incident to talk about how they feel individually and to give their perspective. With this, it becomes easier for mental health professionals to address the most concerning aspect of each incident and focus on it.

Departments need to be more thorough on post incident analysis and not assume that after an incident, everyone is ok. It is easy for people to avoid the subject because it sits heavy on some people, but if it's never discussed then that gives responders more of a reason to put another brick in their backpack. Be proactive and implement an appropriate CISM program into your agency!

Chapter 4

The Best Job In The World

In 2015 I landed my home on a fire department that I wanted to make my permanent career. I had got into a relationship with someone I felt closer to than I had anyone else in my life, and that I could have eventually spent the rest of my life with. Everything seemed to be going well for me. There is nothing quite like becoming part of something so amazing, that you go to work with family, and go home to family too. You are constantly surrounded by family.

Now, in my time I have met people who didn't have that connection with their department. They were surrounded by negative and unsupportive people. So, if you fall part of this, just pay attention because I will be discussing the negative shit too at some point in here.

I wake up at 0530 every third day. I shower the night before so that I can get a little extra sleep in the morning, and I lay out my clothes for the morning. When I get up, I make my bed, brush my teeth, get my uniform on, clean up a bit, put my boots on, belt on, and hat. I grab my keys and I hit the road. My drive is about forty minutes, give or take traffic, and I always arrive at 0630, give or take a few moments.

I was always taught even before this job that if you arrive at 0700 you're late. The crew the shift before may have had a long shift and being there 30 minutes early gives them a chance to go home a little sooner or avoid that last minute call at 0645. So, I make it a point to get to work at 0630 every shift.

If I am on the ambulance, I check my unit thoroughly. If I am on the rescue truck, engine company, or truck company, I check my pack and I look over the unit to make sure I am familiar with where everything is and if it is operational. If it is not, I will attempt to fix it or mark it out of service. As a paramedic, I spend most of my time on an ambulance. Due to the rise in cost of paramedic tuition, paramedics are becoming harder and harder to find, and as a result of that it puts an extra bit of baggage on our shoulders.

After all units are checked it is kitchen time. Nothing is better than being in the kitchen. It's where stories are told, family stories are shared, and the magic happens. The thinking, the leading, and all the conversations. We eat breakfast and plan out the day. We decide what to train on for the day, or we do something around the station such as clean, organize, or fix something that may be broken.

We eventually must figure out what to cook for dinner. As a lieutenant of mine would say; "The hardest part of our job is figuring out what to eat for dinner." This is very true. Look, we train for fires. We train for rescues, emergency medical calls, wrecks, installation of smoke alarms, you name it. We are prepared for that. For some reason, at the fire house, figuring out what to eat for dinner is a complex task. I feel like that may be an issue for others as well. I could be wrong though.

We head to the grocery store and pick up the needed supplies to cook dinner. Most of the time the engineer cooks. On my shift, sometimes it's the lieutenant, but in some way, just about everyone chips in to do something. Whether it is peeling potatoes, cutting asparagus, tenderizing chicken, making yeast rolls or mac and cheese, or just making coffee, most of us are in the kitchen if we're not on a run. The ambulance crews eat first, the suppression crews eat second, and the officer eats last. The rookie does the dishes, and if there is no rookie, it's whoever gets to the sink first. Believe it or not, we fight over the dishes. I take pride in doing the dishes, not to mention I was a dishwasher on the weekends at the age of 15. It was my first job, so when I am on the dishes, I like to stay there. I was always taught as a kid that the cook never does the dishes. I don't cook too often at the fire house, so I'm usually the first one at the sink.

Each one of us enjoys our job. What job can you go to and get paid to do some of the fun things we do on the job? What job can you walk into a house on fire, put it out, and come out and bust balls with your coworkers? This one! What job can you see some of the craziest and funniest shit and have to fix the problem? This one!

What job can you sit around a table at during down time, and tell jokes to each other while drinking a soda and playing cards? This one! What job do you get thanks at, when you help someone? This one. We get to sleep in a comfortable bed at night if we are not on a run, we get people who bring us cookies and cakes, and kids to come play on the trucks. I mean, it truly is the best job in the world when you look at all the great things it offers. But what makes it the best job in the world is your crew. The comradery, the trust, the love, the brotherhood.

I never would have expected the love and support that my department has given me. Of course, we have people we may not agree with, but we will always risk our lives to save theirs. I have been so lucky as to have had the best leaders and seniors to help guide, shape, and support me. In return, I do my best to do the same to those younger than me, and my brothers and sisters. The best part of the job is when you can wake up in the morning and be excited to go in to work. If you don't have that feeling, you need to start to look at yourself and look at the people around you because there may be something wrong that needs to be addressed.

A negative department is not a department that you need to grow in. It will only fill you with more problems, and even more problems when you have a problem but no one to talk to about it. Whew, that was a breathy explanation, but you get my drift, don't you? Look, I'll break it down for you, just in case.

This book is about living through the darkness. We all will be faced with darkness in our lives, but we need to learn how to live through it. Everyone faces darkness in their lives, but we are extraordinary people who do extraordinary things and hold an extraordinary position in an extraordinary field. Yes, lots of extraordinary explanations here! But, because of what we do, we may be faced with more things than the average everyday worker outside of our field. Because of this, we may be faced with more stressors, more traumas, more mind boggling and fucked up shit that no one should see. This is a norm for us in our profession, but not a norm for the human race. Everyday people don't see the shit or do the shit that we do.

What is normal? There really is no true answer to that, but for me, normal is what my baseline of goodness is. My moral compass, the reason why I am here, my goals in life, and how I treat myself and other people. My honesty, integrity, empathy, compassion, wit, etc. What is abnormal to your normal? Look at that.

When you notice that you are not what you think you use to be, and it's not in a good way, there is an issue that needs attention. If you are on a department that thinks your problem is not a problem, maybe they are part of the problem.

One of the best things about our job, and that has been a noble title in this field, in the brotherhood. The brotherhood is dying all across the country. We are getting wrapped up in social media negativity in the service. Arm chair quarterbacking other departments, other firefighters. I know, I have been a part of that and it's something I am not proud of. We are getting wrapped up in clicks at work. Arguing about which shifts are better and picking on the shitty shift with the shitty firefighters and the shitty leadership. I've been guilty of that too, and it was all based-on assumptions. It wasn't until I reached the lowest point of my life, that I realized how true the brotherhood could be. I felt a close connection with my shift, but I felt distant from some of the others. It was all based on assumptions. However, if you have reached a low, or are even realizing that you have a problem, and no one is there to help you, or shames you, you need to look somewhere else. Burn that bridge my brothers and sisters, because that will only bring you further down than you already are.

A perfect example comes from a brother of mine in another state. He is an 18-year veteran of the fire service and has been through so many things and seen so many things in his career. As a result of his previously undiagnosed mental health and substance abuse issues, it took a toll on his marriage as well. He had the guts to get help and he did it all on his own, not just once, but twice. When he did that, the rest of his department called him weak, and didn't support him. His name was drug into the dirt, and he was afraid that he would not be welcomed back at that department to finish his career until retirement.

That is a negative environment to be in. The brotherhood should support you in your worst times, and in your best times. That's one of the reasons why this has always been the best job on the earth. A proactive department will help you grow, not bring you down.

I have heard stories from several men and women who were labeled as weak, because their backpack got so full and heavy that they couldn't carry it anymore. It was so easy to carry their brothers or sisters when they were down, carry a victim who had fallen ill or hurt, but can't carry themselves. It's so easy for others to call 911, but the stigma of us being weak among our own brothers and sisters who are supposed to be there to help one another, leads us to believe that there is no 911 for ourselves. I'm here to tell you that there is. You just have to look in the white pages of the right phonebook to find it. There is hope, I promise you that.

I believed for so long that I would be labeled as weak, or I would be shamed out of the department that I absolutely loved, if I told them that I needed help. It got to the point where I didn't care what they thought. I was nervous, but I knew I needed to do something. If by me doing something, meant someone else recognizing that they too need to do something, then not only was I going to save my own life, but maybe influence others to save their own lives too. Think about that for a moment. Let that sink in. It only takes one person to change the minds of thousands, if not hundreds of thousands. With 30% of firefighters in America having post-traumatic stress disorder (PTSD) at the moment this book was written, it can mean saving the lives of even just one of the over 100 firefighters or paramedics that die by suicide yearly in America. 1 out of every 5 firefighters suffer from PTSD. Look around your department. Look at the firefighter sitting or standing next to you. Look at yourself in the mirror. You are your brother's keeper. Take care of yourself and your crews.

We need to continue to strive to keep this job the best job in the world. We are so proactive on cancer awareness today, even more so after the events of 9/11/01, but we really need to be focusing on mental health as well and substance abuse. They are both killing our brothers and sister all across the country in epic proportions. How many more of our brothers and sisters have to die before we finally take a stand and put a stop to the stigmas?

Acting as interim EMS supervisor.

Chapter 5

Relationships – The Ins And Outs

I am in no way an expert about relationships, not one bit. But what I can tell you is that when I finally found the person that I wanted to spend my life with, it sure all started making sense when I was beginning to see the relationship fall apart. The information that I am going to be covering in this book comes from not only myself, but many sources that I have encountered during my struggle and my recovery. I hope that this will give you more of an insight to the problems that can arise in relationships when you are struggling with your own battles.

Often times, we feel like we have found someone who can love us unconditionally, and who will always understand our wants and needs. If you are anything like me, you may have already posted the warning label about yourself to your better half. That warning label advises them that you are a firefighter, and that you have good days and bad days. It advises them that you are very passionate about your job. There is a lot of work that comes with being in love with a firefighter. In fact, a lot of us find ourselves dating other healthcare professionals, or even other state workers such as teachers. It leaves us room to discuss the troubles on the job with an understanding of each other. Sometimes however, that can turn bad. No matter what you two have in common, there is always room for a disagreement.

I've dated a broad range of people, including other firefighters, paramedics, social workers, and other healthcare professionals. I've also dated people who were not anywhere close to my field of service work. I've found that me personally, my longest relationship was with someone in which we had no common job practice. I think I may have found the reason as to why that relationship suffered. There's one thing I have learned, and one thing that was very hard for me to outgrow. It's something I am currently struggling with but will forever be improving on; separating your work life from your home life.

Separation of Work and Home Life

When we go to work, we engage in things that the lay person should not engage in or see. Our lives are completely different than most people's lives when it comes to the duties required for our job. There are days of satisfaction and there are days of sadness. Some of those days of sadness are so terrifying that when you go home, it's often hard to communicate with your loved ones because you have so much going through your head that you don't want to make your family worry about you. That's just one of a dozen reasons we sometimes choose to not talk about the job at home.

Now, talking about your shift or tour at home is not the only problem. How many of us go away for a few days or even a couple weeks at a time for fire schools, conferences, or specialty training programs? How many of us go to the National Fire Academy for 10-day classes? How about watch videos on YouTube at home, read fire books at home, or constantly critique the latest episode of the emergency service TV show that's on your television at home? I know I have, and I know several other people that have and that still do all of those things. How do you think your significant other feels when all you do is focus on fire department stuff? Here's an even better one. How often do you talk about fire department stuff, excluding the calls you have been on?

If anyone has ever heard their significant other say, *"All you ever talk about is fire stuff"*, you may have a problem brewing that you don't even realize. Now, this may not be an issue you are having but I am still going to discuss it. For us, being a firefighter is a noble profession. We love it, and if we don't love it, well you need to find another profession. Anyway, we love it, but it should not define who we are as a person deep down inside. You may have a title of being a firefighter, a paramedic, a police officer, a dispatcher, or a soldier, but that title does not define you. That's just a job title. You are you! You are John, or Sam, or Sarah, or Mike, or whatever your name is. You are a man or a woman who has feelings, wants, and needs. You are a man or a woman who has beliefs, and heart, and passion. You may have a passion for the job, but that does not make you who you are. Do you understand that? Here, let me dive in a little for you.

When you go to work, you are expected to know the job and do the job well. You are expected to take risks for the goodness of others. You are expected to hold the hand of an elderly lady when she asks you to, because she is lonely. You are expected to ladder a window to help a person who is stuck on a porch of their house that is on fire to bring them to safety. You are expected to carry yourself in a professional manner during your whole shift. You are expected to do station duties to keep it clean and neat. You are expected to listen to your superiors when given an order, or when they are giving advice. Now turn that to when you clock out and go home. You are expected to be the boyfriend, girlfriend, husband, or wife, that takes that role well. You are expected to take risks for the goodness of your significant other. You are expected to hold and love them unconditionally. You are expected to listen to them when they want to talk to you and have an open mind while not interrupting. You are expected to do your part in taking care of the house and/or kids or pets. Do you see where I am going?

Your significant other may ask you how your day is at work, but they may not be emotionally ready for you to explain all the gruesome details of the shift. Don't throw that type of stuff at them unless they have verbalized that they are ready to hear that sort of stuff. This is a good time to communicate your wants and needs, as well as see what their wants and needs entail. Find out if they are willing to listen to the stories about your troubled shifts, but don't take it in a bad way if they say they don't want to hear the details.

Maybe get into the routine of letting them know that when you say that it is a *"bad shift"*, that someone may have died, or that things may not have gone as planned. Get into the routine of telling them that a "*good shift*" means that everything went well, and no major incidents occurred, or that a "*great shift*" means you may have saved a life or a structure. Some people are not ready to hear all the details, and you may need to try and find out what your significant other wants to hear from you, ahead of time and maybe find a happy medium of communication for the both of you that you can work with. Perhaps maybe advising them of certain emotions that you may be having, and how they can be supportive to you when you feel those emotions.

Your Backpack

Sometimes home life gets a little more complicated than we seem to realize. We tend to distance ourselves in order to protect ourselves and the people around us. Remember how I talked about that backpack? Anytime we have a problem, we tend to put it in the backpack and forget about it? Well, that's fine and all, but what happens when you can't put anymore shit in that backpack? That backpack is a form of support for you. You feel comfortable putting all that shit in that backpack. Yeah, it's ok... wait! No, it's fucking not ok. Not ok at all. Let me explain something here, and don't be getting all huffy puffy right now about what I am saying, just read it.

You put a bunch of shit in a backpack. A shit ton of weight gets added and not only can it structurally not support the weight, but there is not enough room. The stitching comes undone and now the zippers become torn and broken. Shit starts falling out. It starts falling out everywhere you go. You pick up the shit that has fallen out, and you put it on the table, the desk, the chair, everywhere for someone else to see. Someone else is seeing all the problems that you have kept tucked away in that damn backpack of yours. Now, your significant other comes home. They start to see the problems you have been hiding. Some of those problems are scary problems, and now they're scared. They may fear you, or they may be fearful for you. Either way, they feel fear. Fear that came from problems that you hid, because you didn't want to bring them into your problems.

At work your coworkers find those problems that you left on the truck, on the ambulance, on the kitchen table, or on the computer desk, and they start seeing a change in you. Some of them may ask you what is wrong, and you usually reply with *"nothing is wrong, I'm ok"*. There is a stigma that you don't want to be attached to because of your own fear. Your fear of rejection. Rejection from friends, family, and loved ones. I must tell you, I have experienced this first hand, and it took me finally realizing that shit was falling apart, to tell that stigma to fuck off and go get help. Ill share a small tale.

I have always worried about other peoples wants and needs. I felt it necessary to make everyone happy and place myself last. I was happy with making other people happy, but in the slightest moment that I didn't achieve the goal I set out for, I started to dislike myself. I felt like I wasn't enough. Stress took its toll on me, and then it started to take a toll on my relationship. The relationship that I valued every moment of, but then realized I was not being as supportive as I thought I was, and not being a good enough listener.

I lived my work, on and off the clock. I needed to separate it from home. I was either working too much or talking about it too much. I was either reading a book about my job or watching videos about my job. I would come home after a horrible shift and take my negativity out on my partner. I would immediately assume I wasn't good enough at my job, and as a result I wasn't good enough at my relationship. I would do things to try and get validation of my efforts, and not receive the validation that I thought that I deserved. Then I would get upset that I wasn't doing enough because I wasn't getting thanked or appreciated enough. As a result, I would just work more. I didn't want to be home.

On the days that I would leave work, I would set a goal for myself to have a good day. I would try and start the day by contacting my partner and saying good morning and asking how the night was. If in that moment I was met with anything other than happiness on the other end, I would let it ruin my feelings for the day. This was a constant thing that I struggled with. It got to the point that I felt like I didn't have an outlet. I felt like I didn't have support at home, an ear to listen to, a hand to hold, someone to give me a hug, someone to listen to me, someone to lend their shoulder when I cried. I would try to voice my concern about a few things and immediately be met with resistance. There was no support. It had disappeared.

Now, my partner at the time this started, had their own struggles going on, and more than likely felt the same way. But communication was so piss poor, that we were both being toxic toward one another. I wanted things to work out and I wanted to know what we could do to make things better and find a happy medium, but I was met with resistance. I felt horrible.

At work, I was making mistakes, I was getting an attitude, and I was beginning to not enjoy my job. I was forgetting the slightest things, making stupid decisions, and losing the positivity that I once had. It got to the point I was trying to find someone to come in and cover me so I could leave. It was when my partner on the ambulance asked me if I would be better off just being home, and I stated that it didn't matter if I was home or at work, I just didn't want to be at either. I was unhappy with myself. I was unhappy no matter what environment I was in. I couldn't figure out why. My mind was always racing with so many thoughts. I had negative thoughts, thoughts about deadlines to projects I had to meet, thoughts about meetings I had to attend, training I had to do, so many things. I often described it as an old black and white television, that when I turned it on and there was no cable, there were black and white lines with that static sound. No pictures, no nothing.

I stuffed so many things in my backpack, that I came home from being in Maine for a week dealing with my mother's estate after her death, and I completely lost control of my mind to the point of psychosis. Yes, psychosis. I had a dissociative moment. For the second time in a couple of months I had gotten angry over something as minute as a toothbrush, that I got mad, only this time I was mad enough that I was attempting to kill myself when I didn't even have the idea of dying in my head. I ended up in an argument that was very much so a blur, and near our spare bathroom with my M&P shield in my hand near my head. When I was back in the moment, I was so upset with myself and confused at the same time. I didn't know why I had my pistol in my hand, and my partner was pulling on me to try and relinquish me of my weapon. I dropped the mag and racked the slide to eject the round in the barrel. I was afraid that my partner pulling on me would cause me to have an accidental discharge. I handed the weapon over and fell apart afterwards. There were several moments during that incident that I had no recollection of. I knew something was wrong. I knew it was time to get help.

Psychosis is real. In a relationship it can be destructive and it can be extremely dangerous to you and your partner in life. Psychosis is when you lose your sense of reality. Nothing seems real. People have committed suicide and more than likely were like me, never really wanting to go that route. But their minds were so convoluted that they didn't know any better. When you have a loved one mention to you that you were spaced out, or were not *"there"*, this could very well be an episode of psychosis, or a disassociate moment. I wasn't there folks! I didn't know what the fuck I was doing and I sure as hell didn't want to die. My mind was just racing so much that I was gone! I snapped! My bag was so full that everything fell out. Everything fell out on the floor of that bedroom and my partner saw it all.

I saw the fear in their eyes in a way that I will never forget. I saw a fear that killed me deep inside. I never want to hurt anyone. I am full of love, respect, compassion, and honesty, and knowing that I hurt someone that I was supposed to have loved and respected absolutely tore me apart. I realized I can't truly love this person. I can't truly love this person until I can love myself. Because by hating myself I am only radiating the negativity to every person that is around me. As a result of my hurting I am hurting other people. You treat other people the same way you are used to treating yourself in one way or another. You just have to recognize that negativity, stop it in its tracks, and channel that into something positive. By doing that, you will radiate positivity, and those people who are positive themselves, will automatically be attracted to the positivity that you radiate. See how that works? Have I mentioned *"birds of a feather?"* They flock together!

Tending To Your Flower

For a relationship to grow, it's like a flower. I read a book by Trent Shelton, called _The Greatest You_, during my recovery. He talked about how a flower requires a special kind of soil in order to grow. Occasionally there are seeds that get dropped into that soil, and those seeds try to kill that flower with the weeds they produce. In order to keep that flower alive, it requires care. You must pull those weeds out, water it, provide nutrients, and give it sunlight. The same thing goes for your relationships. In order to get what you want out of it, you must get rid of those weeds that are destroying the relationship and find out which nutrients you need to introduce to it to make it a lustrous flower. It needs to be tended to with compassion in order to grow. Just think about that.

Another thing to remember, is you cannot love someone enough to change who they are as a person. Love itself, cannot change how your significant other looks at you, talks to you, or behaves. It does not dictate their actions. You cannot change someone else to be how you want them to be, no matter how hard you try. You need to think about your wants and needs, and if they cannot meet those wants and needs that you are looking for, you need to move on to where your needs are being met. Remember, this is all about you. You have to love you, and by loving you, you need to make sure you are getting the nutrients yourself that you need in order to grow.

Another thing to remember is that you also need to be flexible with some things. Sometimes we don't get everything that we want. Wanting and needing are two different things. Needing means you require certain things to survive. Things that are not optional. Things that you literally cannot live without. Wanting means that there are things you would prefer, that make you happy, or fill a void, but those need to be negotiable, and realistic. You must have wants and needs that are realistic and achievable. Expecting to get married to a famous musician or movie star is unrealistic. Expecting to be the happiest person 24 hours a day and 7 days a week is unrealistic as well. We have feelings, and feelings fluctuate. We just need to learn how to cope with those feelings and channel them into something positive. Be realistic.

Moving On, Creating New Friendships &
Relationships

Again, I am no expert on relationships. If I was I don't think that I would have had failed ones, but then again, the only reason why I believe I do is because I feel as though I am too focused on thinking that I should be perfect. None of us are perfect, not even me. But I do tend to have better advice than I practice myself. Maybe for once I will practice the advice that I give others. Making yourself available again isn't that hard. I mean, don't jump right on the bandwagon of making commitments, but meeting new people and talking to them is good. People that spark an interest may enjoy your company, but you won't know until you make that connection. Life is worth taking risks on certain things. What is the worst-case scenario? Someone says they are not interested in talking to you, being friends, or dating, if it ever came to that? That's not a big deal. We move on from those. But moving on, making new friends, and dating, is healthy. It gets you out there meeting people, interacting, and will more than likely make you feel good.

Say you find a person you enjoy being around, and they enjoy being around you. Even if you only get to see them once in a blue moon, that's time you both enjoy. Don't rush it. Talk to them. Now is a chance for them to get to know you. Be honest with them ahead of time. I always tell people that I come with a warning label. I don't tend to intentionally break people's hearts, I am honest, and I do enjoy sharing my time with friends and loved ones. However, I am a firefighter. And with that sometimes comes caution. Our field seems to spark infidelity, but I don't personally fall into that category, and you shouldn't either. Dating a firefighter or a paramedic can be very rewarding. I am not saying that because I am one, I am saying that because we tend to give a lot to people. We know what sacrifice is and have empathy and compassion.

As for infidelity, this can go so far as to, how I put it, look at the menu but not order from it. If you are unhappy in a relationship, you need to communicate the reasons why with your partner, and come to a solution. Neither of you will be helping the situation by cheating or even thinking of cheating. This is extremely unhealthy and toxic for you and them. It is easy to fall into the category of infidelity in order to fill that void that we are not getting from home. Don't do it! Part of living through the darkness means that when we are in dark places, we learn to overcome that darkness and bring light to the problems that make us less than happy.

Those of us who have suffered with PTSD, anxiety, or depression, need to make sure that those people who are close to us know that. But they need to know that those diagnoses don't make us who we are. Just like I mentioned before, it's just a thing we must work with daily, and if under control with medication and therapy will be just as wonderful of a person without them. It can sound scary to some people but someone who truly enjoys and supports you will understand.

I had planned to make new friends outside of the emergency service field, and that is something that I will continue to work on. I am not worried about how many I make or if I make any at all, but that is a goal I have set for myself. Sometimes friends and relationships outside of your field are even more healthy. That goes to help you separate work and home. Having friends that can converse with you with things besides work, is a positive thing for you. You need to have that kind of separation. I am not saying that you don't need to have friends in the service, but you can learn something from someone in a different field the same way they can learn from you.

Accepting Rejection

Part of going out and finding new friends and making new relationships will involve rejection. Remember when I discussed wants and needs. You have to remember that other people have those wants and needs too. That means that if someone else does not feel like they want you or need you, then you need to respect that. Don't beat yourself up over it, just move on. I promise you that you will make new friends and you will find new relationships in time. No one should be in a hurry. Take your time! Time is like having a product made of good quality, you get what you pay for. You come before anything and anyone else.

Time is everything. You won't be able to adapt to changes in your life overnight. We must work on those constantly right? Yeah. Same goes for marriages and such. You will always have to work for it. Making sure your fitness level stays on par, you need to work for it. Keeping your house nice for your family, you work for it.

Nothing is handed to you over night. Everything that is valuable to you will take time and hard work. Hard work is the key to a long life and survival.

People will reject you. That's part of life. People have their own beliefs, just as you do. Can you think of a time in your life where someone wanted to be a friend, or someone wanted to date you and you said no? We all can, and if you can't, then either you haven't experienced life long enough, or you're bullshitting yourself, and me. So, let's cut the shit, and if someone isn't into you, then cool. Move on but be bold and have confidence. No one wants someone that looks like they don't have their shit together. Stand tall, stand proud, keep a smile on your face and confidence and compassion in your heart, and you will be surprised what you can accomplish, but most of all, don't be fake about it. Honesty is the best policy.

Forgiveness

Oh shit, here comes that word we all dread; forgiveness. This is going to be quick and to the point, and is very important to your wellbeing. No, this does not mean that you necessarily go out and ask for it or even give it for that matter. It is a little more than that and I will give you a couple of personal examples.

After I learned about forgiveness, I understood that you can still remember the horrible incidents that lead you to believe that you could never forgive someone. I also learned that sometimes people have their own battles and will never forgive you for something you may have done to hurt them. So with that being said, I don't expect people to forgive me and I don't expect people to accept me forgiving them.

I had a partner one time in which I believed our relationship was good. We hardly ever fought, we worked together well, and we had fun. I met their parents, enjoyed my time with them, and the relationship felt healthy. We had agreed to move into a house rather than the duplex that I rented, and my partner had paid the deposit for the house and began moving stuff out. I was waiting till my 30 days were up before I left, and my partner was fixing things in the house to prepare for my arrival. Last minute, I was told we were splitting up, and I had no time to find a place to live. I was literally out of a home. On top of that, I was denied the opportunity to work for a fire department that I wanted to work for because of my past and poor written test scores, and my financial problem was out of proportion at the time.

I found a storage unit and a friend helped me move everything into it. I packed a bag full of clothes and shower supplies and lived out of my vehicle. I showered at work, and eventually started to sleep on the couch. I did this for quite some time until a friend offered me to come stay with them. I stayed with them for a year or so until I got my path built up the way I wanted, and I moved out. I hadn't talked to my ex more than a passing by hello, in quite a few years. Now, you may be wondering how a person like this can be forgiven. Let me explain it.

When you constantly see the person, hear of the person, or come across something that reminded you of the person, you are immediately brought back to when you were hurt. Those emotions have grabbed ahold of you because you have chosen to let them control you. You are letting something that happened in the past control your present and future. Can you change what happened then? No. Is that event affecting me today as I write this book? No. I shouldn't have had to go through intensive therapy to know that! That is common sense. But, learning about forgiveness has opened a whole new door for me, and it can do the same for you. This goes for friends and intimate relationships as well as yourself.

I got a message from this person while I was in therapy offering an ear if I needed one, and telling me that I was a strong person for making the step to better myself. This made me think about the past for a moment and what was done to me, but that now would be a good time to let go of the past since I was recovering. I forgave them. I told them I forgave them, and that we were both different people back during that time. I know this made that person feel better knowing that I was hurt, but that I wasn't going to let it control my future. Not long after being released from my recovery center, we sat and talked for a few hours as though it was the good days again. I didn't forget the incident, but I did forgive them. We all make mistakes.

The incident that led me to get help, where I pulled a weapon on myself, led me to want forgiveness from my most recent partner. Now, we cannot expect forgiveness if we ask for it. And we cannot expect forgiveness if we hope for it. We can only be open to receive it, but not dwell that it will happen. Instead, we need to recognize the mistake or mistakes that we made, learn from them, and learn to forgive ourselves.

How I felt about myself when that happened was not good. I was disappointed in myself, sad, and scared. I knew I hurt my partner greatly, and also had a lot of guilt for the feelings they had, and the fear that I instilled in them during that dangerous and life threatening moment. After learning about forgiveness, the same concept applied. I made a mistake and I learned from it, not to repeat the same mistake, and I forgave myself. I don't need to constantly beat myself up over an incident that I cannot rewind and delete.

When I finally met with my partner face to face, and learned about their feelings and the emotions that ran through their mind, I kept in my own mind that I may never receive forgiveness from them for the incident, and I came to accept that. However, I apologized for the situation that happened and empathized with their emotions. When I was done listening to how their felt, I replied with,

"I hope that one day you can find it in your heart to forgive me for the pain that I have caused."

Something about that statement, and about me forgiving myself, made me feel like a better person. I had a wonderful feeling that came over me.

Finding the time to forgive others can do wonderful things for you. Remember though, that you don't always have to verbally forgive someone. It is about mentally forgiving them, or yourself. If you can verbally do so, then great! But also remember that others may not accept your forgiveness. That is not your problem, that is their own problem. They may be fighting with their own demons as well, and that is not your problem. You did what was right, and getting into this practice can bring you great joy.

With all that being said, grab a piece of paper and write down the list of people in your life who have hurt you and how they hurt you. Also write a list of people who you have hurt and how you have hurt them. Make it a priority to slowly start forgiving the people you have hurt, and forgiving those who have hurt you. Remember, you can forgive and not forget.

Chapter 6

Isolation, Stress, and Wellness

Often, those of us who are struggling within ourselves begin to lose interest in the things we once loved to do. Our outings with our family start to dwindle down. The fishing trips you planned with your kids suddenly don't happen. And when you had events planned with friends, you found yourself coming up with some excuse to avoid going. You don't want to leave the house, and you sleep in later. You feel tired all the time, don't get adequate sleep, and the excuses start piling up. Your spouse asks you what's wrong and you assure them that nothing is wrong, then your arguments begin. Do any of those sound familiar?

I had always been an outgoing person. I was energetic, comical, and loved meeting people. I absolutely loved meeting new people and making new friends. I never hesitated to initiate a conversation. I would be shy sometimes, but generally I was an extremely happy person all of the time. It took effort to make me mad, aggravated, sad, or even angry. I was always going somewhere to do something in hopes of meeting new and exciting people.

I loved to travel. I loved traveling all over the country experiencing the scenery and enjoying mother nature. I was always an outdoor person, engaging in some kind of outdoor sport or activity. That is how I spent most of my time during my childhood years. I was in martial arts, played softball and soccer, and was an avid inline skater and skateboarder. Mom would take me camping, fishing, and hiking all over the north woods. I built a tree house with friends in the woods and built lean-tos. We would make tea from natural tea leaves that we would find in the woods, pick fiddleheads, and boil water on the fire pit we created.

Over the course of three to four years, my activities that I use to love doing started to fade. I would lose interest in one activity, and then another, and another, and another, until all my previous activities were just taken over by some lame ass excuses. Then, in exchange, I was taking on new activities that didn't involve me leaving the house.

I began restoring leather fire helmets, creating custom wood items, and doing graphic design, all of which are very time consuming and detail-oriented projects. I was getting overwhelmed with orders to the point that I began to add on more stress. I was spending more time on my projects and less time on myself and especially my relationship. I would always have a project due the next day or two and would be plugging away at my projects in the shop. I knew it was getting bad when my partner said to me,

"You should go out and meet some new friends and get out and enjoy time without me."

They were absolutely right. I needed to make some new and more positive friends. Friends that didn't work in my line of service. I mean, they went out with their friends and I would stay home working on projects. I would try to make it a point to go somewhere but would just come up with an excuse not to go.

Some other friends of mine planned a big

camping trip with our RV's. I had reservations for the site and so did about four of the families of my other friends. I got there, backed the camper in, plugged up and plugged in everything, unloaded the cooler and such for the fridge and walked over to help the others. We had a community of people there in the back loop of a circle, and we were all door to door, or close enough to all converse.

I spent most of my time walking my dog and going to the pond to fish by myself. I would sit for as long as I could and fish until I was pretty sure I had caught all the fish at least once. I would then walk around some more, head back to my camper, and turn in relatively early. I spent more time in my camper, or away from everyone else, and I felt miserable.

This is a perfect example of when I would isolate myself. Looking at what I use to do and what I loved to do. Do you have this problem or something similar? This is a pretty big deal right here. You isolate yourself from everything you possibly can. Can you see a trend yet in the subjects being discussed? Can you relate to any of this perhaps? When everything all adds up we need to start putting the clues together.

There are more bad days than there are good days. The fights at home become more frequent. The laziness at work is getting more and more real. Your motivation to even go to the best job in the world is less and less. Your sex life starts sucking, your love life takes a toll, work life, home life, personal life, life, life, life, and life. Get out of the downward spiral.

Stress does a number to you and can be a factor to your isolation on top of many other things. Cortisol is used in moments when your body's fight or flight mode is activated. This happens when we are under stress or are presented with fear, danger, or a heightened awareness such as being hypervigilant. Our job requires us to be hypervigilant but we have a hard time turning that off. This makes it hard when we are home because we are in the same mode at home. Our spouses and such do not understand.

By your body consistently being in fight or fight mode, this disrupts your body's normal functions all the way to the cellular level. This constant activation leads us to an increased risk of cardiovascular disease, diabetes, mental health problems, weight gain, and sleep problems. These are just a few of the many things that increased stress hormones can do to us. Take a moment and think about how your body has been reacting to the stressful environments that you encounter. How many stressful events do you think you have experienced in your life? How long have you been on the job? How about home stressors or other personal life stressors? Depending on many factors it could be little or it could be a ton.

I discuss quite a few ways to help alleviate problems in your life in this book. One of the big problems you need to take care of is stress. This is usually a root for it all. There are several things that you can do that can help you relax, but again you need the motivation to do so. When you isolate yourself it makes it extremely difficult to have the motivation. If you want to know how you can go about addressing the most important things to get you back on track, I cover that in Chapter 8, but I will mention stuff more than once in this book.

First and foremost, you must get the help you need through therapy. Professional counseling is one of the most important steps you need to take. You need to understand your ailments before you can move forward. One of the other most important things you can do is eat healthy and engage in some sort of physical fitness. Be it running, lifting weights, using a row machine, biking, or anything that can get your heart rate up. If you are not someone for a gym remember you can do outdoor sports too. You can play basketball, soccer, softball or baseball. Anything athletic. You can go hiking or kayaking also! There are so many options. This can help you learn about mindfulness, which I will also be covering.

When you elevate your heart rate for an extended period while engaging in exercise, your body releases endorphins. These endorphins act as a natural high giving us energy and a general feeling of overall wellness and satisfaction. I am telling you, you don't have to like exercising because a lot of people don't. But give it a try. Find something that you can work up a sweat to the point of slight exhaustion, and you will find that you feel good.

I hate running, absolutely hate it, but I played soccer, and I almost never sat on the bench. I was doing consistent interval sprints, up and down the field for an entire game which lasts almost two hours. People would assume that I would be worn out after thirty minutes of sprinting but no. You get what I call a "*second wind*". You get so tuckered out and feel like you can't run anymore, and then all those endorphins suddenly kick in and you're ready to kick ass. In the winter times I didn't like doing cardio outside so I started running on the treadmill. I hate running, but after the first mile I would feel good and run another mile. After that second mile I would feel good and run a third. I would eventually end up running a 5k three times a week, and when I finished I would feel fantastic.

It's not getting addicted to running or lifting; it's being addicted to those endorphins. Not literally, but endorphins act on neurotransmitters in the same way that certain pain medication acts. That's why people have been able to identify the fact that endorphins can help mask pain. You got it, pain. Pain like, I stepped on a nail, pain. So, they act on mental pain too. Do yourself a favor and change that diet of soda, chips and shit, to healthy meals with appropriate macronutrients and drinking that glorious H2O. I know some of you will be like,

"*Oh, but I hate water, it has no flavor.*"

I use to say that. I tried to add flavors and all but it just didn't cut it, so I toughed it out and started to drink water. I set myself a goal. I would take a one-gallon jug and write times on it from the top to the bottom, with a little line. Every hour that I wrote on there, I had to drink that amount of water down to the line. I made it a goal to drink that every single day. Minus having to pee so much that I was pretty sure I may have needed to buy some depends, it helped make me feel full, which made my meal portions smaller, boosted my metabolism, which helped with weight loss, and it improved overall function of healing and other body functions.

Meditation, or mindfulness, is something that we can all do. You do not have to be an expert in meditation or some Zen Buddhist that meditates a majority of the day. Learning about being mindful and/or various ways of meditation, can help ground us in some of our most stressful events. Meditation does not necessarily mean that you need to sit in a position such as the position shown in the chapter image (lotus position) and be quiet. Though that is one way to meditate, that's not always appropriate for everyone.

Meditation can be done in numerous ways.

Sitting alone in an upright and comfortable position, away from people and other distractions, and focusing on your breathing and your body. Nothing or no one else. It can be done walking and doing the same, however paying attention to the feeling beneath your feet, the smell of the air or the breeze across your body. It can also be done through guided meditation, meaning someone speaking to you softly and guiding the movements you make.

These techniques help us learn how to ground ourselves when we begin to feel anxious, or we begin to feel our mind racing or negative thoughts. Stressful or overwhelming moments can be controlled by simple meditative techniques, and can not only help us mentally, but physically as well.

Yoga is another option for some people to engage in. Not only is it meditative, but it is physical as well. You do not have to be an athlete to do yoga. Yoga in group settings is very good too, as you can not only get to know new people but you can also work on meditation techniques in an environment that may normally cause you to be hypervigilant. It's a fantastic activity to engage in because it helps you raise that heart rate, break a sweat, and centers your mind. You can eventually take the techniques you learn and practice yoga in another relaxing environment such as on a mountain, by the ocean, or in another wilderness location.

Learning ways to ground yourself can be a very effective tool for you and your healing as well as growth. Other people will also be able to tell and will absorb your mindfulness and calmness. Tranquility is contagious and I truly know this. The more tranquil you appear and feel, the more others around you may begin to feel that way too. It's as though they see the things they are missing from themselves, in you.

So. set yourself some realistic and achievable goals. I am not putting this all on paper because it looks good or sounds good. I am doing this because it works. I have done it and so have many other people. You need to give yourself that drive, that motivation, that willpower, to kick this shit right in the face and say,

"I'm donewith this bullshit that keeps bringing me dowñ.
Ladies and gentlemen now is the time to burn those rickety ol' dangerous bridges, and to build one out of concrete and steel. One so strong that nothing can

break it down, but only you can hold it up.

I home cook a lot of healthy meals incorporating all the food groups.

7

Depression, Validation, & Living For The Moment

There seems to be this huge stigma of firefighters being considered weak if they admit that they have a problem. Now, I mention this quite a few times in this book that I am not a genius at this shit. I am simply here to tell you my opinion and share some of the education that I have obtained while being in an intensive therapy program. I am also here to tell you the shit I have personally dealt with or have been able to hear from other brothers and sisters in therapy. So sit tight and digest on.

In chapter 8 I discuss growing a pair. This serves for both men and women. By that I mean swallow your pride and tough it out. There is a reason you need to do this. In fact, there are many reasons and I will try to give you some examples as I continue to ramble on here.

We serve the people. The people of these cities, counties, townships and such, all rely on us, and most of the population look up to us. They know that we are there when they need help. We all know that firefighters are called for some of the most obsolete things, but we are all around fixer-upper people. We can do anything. We all have a variety of special skills outside of just fighting fire and providing medical aid.

Some of us are plumbers, constructor workers, engineers, teachers, electricians, auto mechanics, computer technicians, or farmers. That is one thing a lot of fire departments look for in a person when they hire them. What sort of special skills do you have? These special skills come in handy from time to time and in what better place than on the most obsolete calls. Calls that have absolutely nothing to do with firefighting or medical calls. Sometimes we get these calls because people just don't know who else to call. We are here to save the day.

We've been called to fix porches, install air conditioner units, fix electrical outlets that don't work, and even help move groceries and furniture inside a resident's house. This builds trust within the community, and they are happy knowing that we will always be there with a smiling face and a helping hand whenever they need us. Trust is an important thing within the community.

Think about this at your fire house. What sort of trust do you have? Do you have brothers and sisters that you generally feel good around, or do you constantly feel like you must stay on guard? Do you hear them make conversation about people with mental health issues or substance problems in a negative way? If so, there are signs that you may be missing.

Negative signs can make you feel vulnerable and may make you want to isolate yourself from others. You may be quiet on shift, not want to par-take in kitchen chatter, or be negative yourself when it comes to training. You may begin to feel helpless and lonely, or even begin to feel depressed, not wanting to even go to work. This stuff affects your home life too, remember that.

When you start to feel down by the people you are around, this rubs off on your runs too. You start becoming irritable on your runs. Your empathy turns into apathy, and your motivation to stay on the job becomes less and less. I have mentioned in this book that we have the best job in the world. If you wake up and don't get excited about going into work, you may need to re-evaluate yourself and ask yourself why.

During stressful calls, you may not be entirely focused. Remember how the public looks at you? Well, they are still looking at you and if they see a different you in the worst moments than in the good moments, they may have a feeling that you can't handle the job. A lot of the general public think that we are trained to be tough and able to handle the most horrific scenes. That stigma follows along into the fire department too.

Someone once said that stigmas are real, but a stigma is only a negative opinion of what other people think of you or what you think of yourself. It's negative opinion. A stigma is not real unless you make it real, and if you're making it real then you need more positivity in your life. Crush the stigma and take care of you. You are the most important person in this world, not the opinion of someone who is not. A stigma is a label.

Labels are placed on many different things but sometimes don't contain all the ingredients inside the packaging. Get my drift?

By saying that, you need to keep that mentality. If you have a department that thinks that you are any less of a person because you have realized that something is not right inside your heart and mind anymore, than you really need to weigh the odds. There is a quote that I have heard a time or to. You can either get busy living or get busy dying. And believe me, getting busy living is so damn rewarding, you need to jump on that shit.

If someone is keeping you from being the best you, then you need to say goodbye. A great and supportive department will be by your side every step of the way. Who does not want a firefighter on their department who is not afraid to better themselves and be the best person for the job? Just because you have been kicked a few times and have fallen does not mean that you can't heal, get back up, and be stronger.

They say when you break a bone, the new bone growth comes back stronger than before. So, when you are broken down and begin your process of re-growth, you will come back ten times stronger than you were before. Who does not want that? Who would deny that from their line of warriors? Only a failing leadership would deny that from their crew.

Because of all the stress you are going through, you tend to push things under the rug. You think that this is just a phase, and you will get over it in a few days. You think you may just be tired, or maybe taking on too many projects. There is an excuse for everything as to why you won't speak up and make the call.

You may feel lost, confused, or misunderstood. You may be putting a mask on and not even realizing that you are, even more so if other people are constantly asking if you're ok. Ask yourself that question and be honest with yourself. Are you ok? You need to be honest with yourself. You may be good at lying or shrugging off your problems when other people inquire about your wellbeing but don't do that to yourself.

Being in denial is all a part of grieving. I always say that when people are struggling with something or have a problem, in a sense they may be grieving. They may be grieving over the fact that they are not the same person they use to be or feel like they are not the same person that they use to be. You and I both know that denial is something you have when other people inquire. Your responses are, *"I'm ok"*, or *"I'm just tired"*. You have excuses. Excuses, excuses, excuses. You know what they say about excuses? Sure you do, but I am going to tell you anyway.

"Excuses are like assholes. Everybody has them ."

So how about depression? Are you depressed? Just because you are sad a lot does not make you depressed. If you have ever been diagnosed with depression, then you already know what comes with it. You've taken all those pretty tests that give you the answers. Your therapist comes out and says, "Congratulations, you have depression." Well let me tell you the first thing that's wrong there.

One of my clinicians told me once that you do not have depression, you just happen to be depressed. I mentioned this before. You are not your diagnosis. You just feel that way. Do not let any of that control your life or who you are as a person.

For those of you who have not been diagnosed with anything, take a look at some of the things that could make you believe that you may be feeling depressed.

Isolation (Oh wait, I think I talked about that already… let's keep going.)

Fatigue (You would rather sleep then do anything.)

Difficulty sleeping/Insomnia (You toss and turn. It takes you forever to fall asleep, and you never wake up well rested.)

Lack of sexual interest (You don't want sex. Even if the sexiest person walked up to you and made themselves available, you would decline.)

Hopelessness (Not being optimistic, lack of hope.)

Guilt (Feeling like all negative outcomes are your fault.)

Eating habits (Excessive weight loss or weight gain.)

Do any of these click for you? I mean I am not putting every single sign in here, but a few of the common ones, and quite a few of the ones that I have personally experienced. All of them at once is even worse! You have separated yourself from absolutely everything from social atmosphere (external) to health (internal). You really need to check yourself brothers and sisters. This shit ain't no joke and will absolutely drive you into the ground.

Depression does not mean that you are necessarily in trouble. It is the most common mental disorder diagnosis in America, and nearly one out of twelve Americans have it. It can be as the result of many things not just things we see on our job. It can be a family member who has died, someone who has been diagnosed with a terminal illness or a difficult illness requiring a lot of attention. It can be as the result of some form of abuse, or just as a result of lack of self-care causing us to lose any and all ways of coping with life's constant changes.

Several years ago, I was told by a great friend and mediator not to let the little things get me down. I never understood why I let the little things get me down. Then the little things became bigger things, and bigger things, and eventually I found myself in a hole. I felt like no matter how hard I tried to do something the results were never as I wanted them. I use this as a perfect example.

You go home and realize that your floor needs to be vacuumed so you vacuum it and you decide to shampoo it as well. You move all the furniture and everything else off the floor and clean the baseboards while you're at it. It looks perfect. When your spouse or better half gets home, they don't even notice. You are missing the validation.

The same thing happens at work too. If you are not getting validated at work or at home, then you end up putting yourself in a hole that is hard to get out of. You feel unappreciated and you can begin to become extremely aggravated. By becoming aggravated you almost put yourself in a sense of desperation, making you try harder and harder to get the attention you want, and then getting extremely angry when you never end up reaching a goal you have.

You may get to the point where you are on social media more often than you should be. You are constantly on it, making several posts a day and spending more and more time trying to see how many "likes" you have on your posts. You are on your phone during special events when you are in the company of others, and rather than focusing on being in the moment, you are more focused on trying to receive attention on Facebook or other social media outlets. This is a perfect example of someone who is lacking self-love, and the need to seek validation elsewhere.

Stephen Thayer, a clinical psychologist, stated in an article by BYU,

"When we stay in our private, online, social worlds, we miss out on the social crucible of face-to-face interaction that forges emotional resilience and character. Pandering for 'likes' on Facebook or Instagram does little more than feed an addiction to validation."

People often say that social media kills friendships and relationships, and that can be very true. My last domestic partner would constantly be on their phone refreshing the social media sites, even while trying to spend quality time together. We are so focused on everyone else. Everything is at the touch of our finger tips and it's as though we have become detached from the real world.

While I was in treatment, my cell phone was taken from me. Internet access was blocked from social media pages. We could use our cell phone an hour at a time, three times a week. Most people only had enough time to pay their bills. Me, I used it to research ideas for my book and to find positive quotes to share. I never posted that I was in a treatment facility, asked for prayers, or good vibes. I kept that part of my life personal to me. It was no one else's business where I was and it was not something that needed to be anyone else's business.

On weekends we would go to scenic sites around the area. Some of these sites are world famous sites, scenic, and admirable. Guess what we didn't have to take pictures with? Our phones. We didn't even have cameras. No way of truly capturing anything in a photo for memory. You were just there, looking, watching, or doing, alongside other people just like you.

I never truly realized how amazing it was. As I looked around, more people were too focused on their phones than experiencing the moment that they were in.

When watching something, they would video it. Not truly capturing it with their eyes, but through the small screen in which lenses would capture the video as you watched it record.

The first time I went out, we all took a nice drive around Washington DC and then went to Arlington National Cemetery. We walked into the information center and waited as each person used the latrine before heading out. We had no plans to take a bus or a tour, but just to walk around in peace, and a chance to be mindful as we were there.

We walked to where the Tomb of the Unknown Soldier was and watched the changing of the guard. This was something that I had always wanted to do and was something that was on my bucket list. It was a moment that I truly enjoyed. I stood there in the moment, respecting the discipline instilled in each soldier and the dedication of such a noble duty. I was at peace there and smiled softly.

Looking around, I didn't see one single person in the moment. Each and every person there was videotaping the event or snapping photos. I was truly in shock, in a positive way for a few reasons. I knew that the help that I was getting while in treatment was working. Just seeing these things was like looking in a mirror and seeing myself in the past.

I love taking photos, and now that I think about it, there had been several times where I wasn't in the moment. Where I was just there to snap photos and carry on. Mind you, there have been many times that I have been in the moment, but after seeing this I had a new respect for being in the moment. Being able to truly ground yourself and surround yourself in so many positive things is of the utmost importance to truly living through any darkness.

I never truly realized how I may have hurt someone because I was too focused on looking on my phone. I watched videos and read articles on my phone all the time. Though I wasn't constantly glued to social media; I did seem to appear to rely on my phone a lot. Sometimes I would leave it in my vehicle just to get away or because I didn't want to answer the phone or texts that kept coming in. Those were the wrong reasons though.

After being released from my treatment, I took a month to travel and do things that I loved to do. I drove over 3,000 miles and visited many places and many people. Of the places that I visited, I stopped at the 9/11 museum in New York City. So many people were there throughout the day. It was an emotional experience and I watched people taking pictures of all the artifacts and structures in the museum. I never took my phone out. I made sure to practice being mindful and living in the moment. That moment was filled with emotion that I do not believe I could have felt had I been on my phone.

We should honestly look at our use of technology as a way that distracts us in a potentially negative way. We should look at it and possibly limit our time on it. Like anything else, schedule a time to be on the phone or schedule a time to be off the phone. Be in the moment and live in the moment.

Live for each moment, not for each day. The day is never promised. Tomorrow is never promised. But the moment you are currently living in is already being lived. So, live it, breathe it and be a part of it. Moment by moment. Ground yourself and be mindful... and while we live for the moment, and not for the day, we can think of one happy thought to make us smile every moment of everyday, and that's 960 moments. Make 960 memories that bring you a smile and add an extra

960 for reserve. When you run out of positive memories to fill those moments, make it a goal to make more, and more, and more.

There is a quote from a famous Buddhist monk and author by the name of Thich Nhat Hanh that comes to mind as I mention this. He says,

"People usually consider walking on water or in thin air a miracle. But I think the real miracle is not to walk either on water or in thin air, but to walk on earth. Every day we are engaged in a miracle which we don't even recognize: a blue sky, white clouds, green leaves, the black, curious eyes of a child — our own two eyes. All is a miracle."

These are very true words, but you must believe in them. I find that when I am having a hard time with things going on in life, I go back to being mindful. Practicing mindfulness is not something that you can do in just a day, it takes practice, as I mentioned before. But once you accomplish the task of being mindful, you will be more at ease in your struggles. Learning about ways to be mindful has been a blessing for me and can be a blessing for you too.

Meditating sitting atop Grey's Arch in the Red River Gorge, KY.

8

8 Steps To Achieve The Objective of Being A Happy Fucking Person Again

PTSD, depression, and anxiety, all suck sweaty ass. No one wants to be labeled as the "*weak*" one or the "*emotional*" one. No one wants to be looked at as though you are going to snap and go off on some crazy spree. That's a thought that every first responder thinks, making it more difficult for them to get the help they so desperately need and deserve.

For so many years I put up a wall. I put up a wall of *"I'm so tough that this shit will never bother me to the point I lose control."* Some people could tell when I was upset after a run. Some people knew that certain frequent flyers drove me to the point of near burnout, until one run would make it all worth the effort to keep going with continued empathy. But with all the fatality car accidents, burned bodies, screaming patients, crying children when their parents died, or crying parents when their children died, it came to a point that I couldn't carry it anymore.

It was such a shame that it took my mother dying, my own personal therapist, to realize that I couldn't handle it anymore. I would always talk to my mother and she would listen. It wasn't fair to take all that home, but in the same sense it wasn't fair for me to be so quiet about all of my feelings. Again, I didn't want the most important people in my lives to know the utter grief deep down inside me, even my mother. I use to just tell her that I had a bad fire where multiple people died that we couldn't save, or I would tell her a young man asked me to hold his hand as he was dying, because he didn't want to die alone.

It was simple to talk about "*the job*", but it wasn't simple to talk about how I didn't want to live anymore. That every day I would ponder what this world would be like without me. How I would think it may be a much easier option than to still be here on earth. But I loved life, and I loved the people I had in my life, I just didn't love myself enough.

I used the EAP (employee assistance program) a couple of times to kind of reach out and figure out what was wrong with me. My mind was always racing and I was hyper-vigilant everywhere I went, even when I sat in a vehicle as a passenger. My mind was so convoluted that I didn't know what I was doing most days. I was forgetting the simplest of things, getting angry over bogus shit, and having difficulty sleeping. Nightmares were kind of random and would come on without even talking about the topic in the dream beforehand. I would always be super cautious to loved ones, wondering where they were, afraid they would be in danger somewhere and I couldn't help them. Then, if they were actually in danger and I wasn't there or didn't express my concern, I would have felt guilty for not being there. I felt screwed either way.

EAP never worked. In fact, it was such a disappointment that I finally believed that there was no one who would be able to help me. I was either going to have to suffer with my own mind and thoughts or put a bullet in it to stop the racing. I was trying to get help on my own without no one knowing for quite a while. The only thing that I did was see my primary physician to get prescribed a medication to keep my mind at bay. It felt like it worked fine for about a month or two, but the feeling was starting to come back, and I have since learned that medication will not fix your problem. You need therapy and medication. Productive therapy that is.

It was obvious I was having issues right after my mother died in January of this year. It was also even easier to get by, because everyone would think it was just my mother's death making me upset and not the job. I didn't want people to think it was the job but as I opened up a little more, I slowly let out bits and pieces of my sadness. I finally mentioned whether I was at home or at work that I would still feel the same way. Camping, hiking, kayaking, fishing, hunting; during it all, deep down inside, I was a mess and I didn't know why.

It took me arguing about a damn toothbrush and me pulling a weapon on myself, to realize that this was not me and this was too far. I absolutely needed to get help. I knew I needed to get help. I knew I was a strong person but that I just needed to take off these bricks that were weighing me down. So, I finally did it. It took me years of self-destruction, failed friendships, failed relationships, failing health, and failing ethics, to realize that there were no more options left for me. I had to do something.

I made the call. I got accepted to a program that was specifically for firefighters with mental health issues or substance abuse issues. I was booked for admission beginning on a Monday. I flew to the location with an open mind in front of me and the image in the mirror fading away. My goal was to find out what was wrong with me, learn about it, and get the skills and other necessary tools I needed to carry on successfully, and happily, for the rest of my life.

It was no shock that I was diagnosed with PTSD, but I was also diagnosed with depression and anxiety, which apparently coincides with PTSD. One thing that was drilled into my head, and that I finally accepted, is that I don't have depression, I'm just occasionally depressed. I don't have anxiety, I'm just occasionally anxious. I don't have PTSD, I just occasionally deal with post-traumatic stress. A diagnosis does not make you that diagnosis. I am still Melissa Parker, a firefighter and paramedic that lives in Kentucky, loves to hunt, fish, and be outdoors. A diagnosis does not change who you are. They're just words to describe how you feel from time to time. There are so many things I have learned while being admitted, that it really made me wake up and question,

"Why did I wait so long to get help?"

Whether you go to a facility like I did or not, here are some tips on how you can kill the negativity and achieve the objective of being a happy fucking person again.

Step One: Recognizing That You Come First

It is so easy for people to call for us when they are having an emergency. To each person, right, wrong, or indifferent, that caller on the other line is experiencing an emergency. They call and we come to their aid. But who comes to us when we need help? There is no 9-1-1 readily available for us. No one is pounding on our door asking us to let them in when we are in crisis. No one is forcing entry to make sure we are ok when the phone hangs up, or we stop talking.

Why do I say that? Well, I say that because it takes us to realize that we are #1. We come first. I explained to a clinician just last week in group therapy one simple thing that every single first responder can relate to.

When we first start our trek into the wonderful world of first response, we are taught one thing very well. Scene safety. When we break down scene safety, it is always you that comes first. Your safety first, your partner or crew second, and the patient or victim last.

Now this isn't a time to sit there on your computer screen or cell phone and arm chair quarterback. This isn't a dick measuring contest. these are basic SOPs in almost every single department nationwide. Of course, most of you risk your lives for the goodness of someone else, but the fact of the matter is you watch for yourself first. If someone is trapped in a burning house that's fully involved, you know your risk vs reward is extremely low.

So, think about things before you jump to conclusions here.

You are number one. As hard as it is to swallow that pill, if you don't love yourself, you cannot effectively love someone else. It is impossible. How do you expect to love something if you have no idea what love is? You absolutely must love yourself first, and if you don't, well you better get to working on that. Your relationships suffer, your children suffer, your family suffers, and your friends suffer when you don't love yourself. You may think you put on a good show, I know I did, but it doesn't have very many episodes left before it starts sucking so bad that no one wants to watch it.

It should never matter what anyone else says if you think something needs to be done, and you know it's what is best for you, and you do it. Stop making yourself unhappy. Start making yourself happy fucking person.

Step Two: Grow Some Guts

You are not weak! Just because you have a problem does not make you weak! Get that through your skull. The only people that are weak, are those brothers or sisters who will not accept or support the fact that you need help and are brave enough to get the help yourself. They are supposed to be your support system (and I will mention that later). How can they protect you from dangers on the fire ground or medical calls, but not help protect you from you? They should be supportive all the way, and in return, should feel honored that they stand side by side with someone who is not afraid to ask for help when they need it. Those alone are true traits of a leader.

So, don't look around your firehouse or station and say to yourself, "*I don't want them to think I am weak.*" You need to think for you, not for anyone else. You come first. You, and only you. As I mentioned before, if you have that kind of negativity in your department, you may need to look for a new department. One that will help you grow those guts to make the call.

Step Three: Make The Call

Do not ever withhold the call. You may have friends who can listen but you need someone who is trained and can provide you with what you need. Your friends can be your support network later when you start getting your life back together and moving forward. You will also realize who your friends are when you start this process. It will begin your process of elimination that you will need to consider later. I can get into that too. I'm talking about burning bridges or cutting ties with the negative shit.

There are countless services out there to help guide you on your way or get you the help you need. A few of the resources are listed at the end of this book. You can also go off somewhere quiet and do a google search. That is what landed me in the facility that helped me. So, make the call. You passed the first two steps, and those are the hardest steps. Making the call will begin to pave your road but remember, there is always gravel and work before the pavement is flat and smooth!

Step Four: Don't Give Up

Just like in your line of work, you don't need to give up on yourself. You may run into hurdles while you seek treatment. You may have therapists that you don't like, take medication that does not seem to help, and you may feel like things are not going as planned. Remember, if this was easy then everyone would be doing it; but because more and more people are starting to brave the waves, and are getting out to get help, some things may take a little time.

Things are not supposed to be hand delivered. Remember, your greatest satisfaction comes from when you have great results after hard work, so keep working hard. Hard work will pay off, I promise. I was always taught that if you want something bad enough that you will work hard for it.

I worked very hard to get what I needed. It wasn't just given to me. I took classes on absolutely everything to do with mental health and healing, 7 days a week, and 6 hours a day, for over 30 days. That compiled with EMDR (Eye Movement Desensitization and

Reprocessing), Hypnotherapy, Physical Therapy, Individual Therapy, and CBT (Cognitive Behavioral Therapy). Of course this was an intensive program, but you continue individual therapy for as long as you need to. You need both therapy and medication to get you where you need to be. One without the other is just asking for catastrophe. I've been there too.

So, ride the hills or waves, but remember that they eventually will settle down. No storm only lasts one minute. Big storms always require rebuilding. This is just your way of obtaining the tools so you can build it correctly. You can't just duct tape everything!

Step Five: Get Away

It is extremely hard on people emotionally to be separated from loved ones and family. It is even more so hard to get time off from work. But, part of getting help involves healing, and healing requires a healthy atmosphere. Being at home, work, around wives, husbands, children, girlfriends, boyfriends, or stress, inhibits your growth. Wrapping yourself up in social media or television, also inhibits your growth. You need to get away, and I don't mean by isolating yourself.

A good mental health facility will help rebuild you as you. They will help you focus on you but will not exclude your family from growth as well. Many of these places offer counseling for families and spouses. This is part of the rebuilding process. You will learn how to listen and how to communicate. You will walk out a better communicator and listener.

When you are going through problems just remember, your families are going through them with you. They have seen the changes in you. They have had to suffer with you while not completely understanding what your suffering is from. You have gotten to the point that you feel like no matter what you do, your family is never happy, no one is ever happy, and as a result you feel unhappy. They know this. Being away to get the help you need to be better also helps them grow as well. They should also be a good support for when you come home with a better understanding of your needs, and with you better understanding their needs.

Getting away does not mean that you pack up your shit and just run from your problems. Getting away means checking yourself into a facility to get the help that you need every day, until you can begin to take those new tools out into the world and try to use them. It's like rebuilding your life back to the way it was before you started having problems. Back to the day where you could laugh and carry on. You did things you loved doing and went places you loved to go to. You smiled more and stressed less.

Step Six: Burn The Old Bridges: Build New Bridges

Friends are great. They stand by your side through thick and thin. Here comes a difficult decision to make and it may be handled in a variety of ways. Negative friends have two options. Either stop being negative when you are around, or stop being your friend. If they're negative, that's a bridge you need to burn. Surrounding yourself with negative Nancy's will only make you a negative Nancy. Surrounding yourself with positive ones will make you more positive! I did mention birds of a feather. You can't work hard to be an amazing and strong person, only to be around those who can bring you back down. You really need to look at that. Those people who are true friends will help you grow in a positive way.

Consider making friends who are not in your profession. You really need this to help you be able to separate your work and your home life. I am not saying that you can't go out with your coworkers but having friends who are not in the profession that you are in sparks different and intelligent conversations. You need that part of work separation in your life. This could also help you be a little less hyper-vigilant.

Shut off the emergency notifications. You should be able to go home and not think about a police car, fire truck, or ambulance. You should be able to hear a siren passing by and continue on your way as though it's just another vehicle. You do not always have to be *"on call"*. Shut off your mobile apps that notify you of calls. Stop watching the horrible emergency television shows. Shut off the work world! I promise, your spouse will appreciate this.

If you volunteer in your spare time, give yourself a schedule of when you will turn your radio or pager on.

Don't do it all day. Give yourself a few hours during the day or evening, or even at night if you work your paid job during the day. Make a schedule of your "*work*" times, both for career job and volunteer, and stick to it for a bit. See how that pans out.

Don't work yourself to death. You may have been the one that worked all kinds of overtime because we know you love the job, but stop. If you are struggling with bills, sit down and calculate your spending and such. Recalculate your budget and go from there. You should not have to work your life away to live. Work to live, don't live to work. Figure out where the problems lie, and work on them. Don't live at work. Your spouse or loved ones need you just as much as you need them. They deserve you coming home to be with them.

Burn a few of the bad bridges and build a few new ones. There are many that you will learn about in time, but here are just a few things you can think of and work on as you ease your way into the process.

Step Seven: Build a Support Network

Kind of goes along with burning bridges. You need a support network. Usually coworkers are a good form but that's for at work. You need a good support network back home too. Spouse, partner, friend, or family; anyone that will be by you 110% of the way, and help you reach your goals. That's a support network. You need that in order to be successful. Build it, you can do that before even going into treatment or therapy! You will always benefit from a great support network. 1 or 2 really good friends, that you know would do anything for you. That is a support network. But those supporters can't be negative! They should be of sound mind themselves and have enough energy in themselves to help you along your path too.

Step Eight: Never Stop The Growth

When you have undergone therapy, and you begin to feel better, don't stop. You can't just wake up and say, "*Oh, I think I feel better than ever. I'm going to stop seeing the shrink and stop my meds*." That is a horrible idea. You must keep getting therapy. You must continue your meds, and then you can ween off medication if suggested by the provider, all while still seeing a therapist and seeing where you go from there. It's like anything else. You took a while to build yourself up happiness and self-love and now you need to slowly release those helpers, to see how you do without them. But always allow the therapist that you see and trust, to help you dictate your needs. Some people need to go to therapy several days a week, some only a couple. Then they go once a week, then twice a month, and so forth. It's always done in moderation and control.

Remember, you worked so hard to get where you wanted to be. Do you want to have to go through all that again if you failed to use the tools that were first given to you? Don't stop growing. Don't stop learning. Keep up the work. Keep up the therapy. You will get there. Just keep telling yourself that. You will get there.

Look, the days of being considered "*weak*" should be simmering down. You are number one, and those people who truly care about you will be those who will stick by you and be your support group. I can't cover absolutely everything, only what I know and what I have done for myself. Surprisingly enough, every single person that I have met in my process, have done the same things in their own way.

You will succeed if you put forth the effort. Life is indeed worth it. There are so many great aspects of life that you have yet to even see or experience. Stick around and see. Things often must sink before they can be found and brought to the surface. Don't be afraid of swimming! Ride that wave and you'll eventually reach the island of paradise and humbleness.

This is a process that you will be working with every single day of your life. Every person on the planet will be dealing with their own struggles every single day. Everyone has a problem, or problems, but some people know how to recognize those problems and begin to ground themselves and become mindful. You can do the same thing. There is no mountain too big for you to climb. Just stick with it. Your family deserves it, your loved ones deserve it, but most of all, **YOU** deserve it. Do it for **YOU** above all else. **YOU** are worth it.

2019 – Shortly after returning home from therapy.

Chapter 9

Religion & Spirituality

There is a saying that there are two things that are not discussed in the fire house. That is religion and politics. Let me hold you up right there for a minute. If you are not religious, you can still gain something from this chapter. You can still be spiritual. Now, spiritual does not necessarily mean that you believe in God. It means that you are concerned with the inner being of yourself. The mindfulness and tranquility of life and your surroundings rather than a physical being or materialistic thing.

Some people turn to faith as a coping mechanism for their despair. Religion, be it Christianity, Judaism, Muslim, Buddhist, or any form of an organized or non-organized religion in which there is a deity or higher power involved, can have ways of making us feel tranquil, loved, or supported. Having that spiritual connection to a deity can serve as an everlasting friendship or love, that can help guide you to a life of peace.

I was baptized Lutheran but never attended a Lutheran church in my life, other than for my baptismal within the first year of my birth. My father was Catholic and would attend the local Catholic mass on some Wednesdays and on Sundays. This was of course when I was younger, and before his alcoholism kept him from going. I wanted to start going to church with him, and I wanted to learn about God.

I remember my mother getting me a book called Little Visits with God. I would sit on the couch at home and read it as a child. My mother got me my own bible, as her mother did for her, and her mother's mother did for her. I still have that bible to this day, but I would read passages as often as I could and found peace by some of the messages I read.

As I got older, and as I got more involved in the line of work that we do, I started to fall away from organized religion and I became more spiritual. I didn't want to adopt one religion and I didn't want to live in one said way. I wanted to enjoy the world for what it was. I wanted to experience what was right in front of me. I wanted to love with no boundary, travel the world with no limits, and treat others in a way that I would want to be treated.

I became so infatuated with the kindness of the way I thought things should be that I never gave myself time to be kind to myself. I was always worried about fixing other people and not myself. Solving everyone else's problems, but continuing to suffer with my own problems, then taking the burden of other people's problems. I was just adding more and more to that backpack of mine. This was not being spiritual. I can't be spiritual if I can't even love myself!

During treatment, we discussed religion and spirituality. It's almost a staple in the mental health programs. Many people in my program were people of religious faith. Many were Christians, and some were Jewish. I have always respected everyone regardless of their religion. I have learned a bit about a bunch of different religions in my travels, and in being in a treatment facility with several denominations.

Some people would turn to God for answers, but the thing that was mentioned by many was that without love for yourself, you can't overcome every obstacle put in front of you. There was a saying that God will not put something in your way that he does not think you can handle. That is a wonderful saying to recognize that you must find inner peace within yourself.

Another thing that is talked about is being mindful. Mindfulness. This comes with a quote that I say about living for each moment, and not each day. Each moment is currently being lived and you can live in it, whereas the day is not guaranteed. Nor is the week, month or year. Being present in the moment is the beginning of understanding mindfulness.

My aunt has been reading Buddhist monk texts and practicing the art of meditation and mindfulness for over 35 years. I never once put the two together until I began treatment. She started me off by throwing some authors at me, and I agreed to learn more about mindfulness and how I could be mindful. I read books by Timber Hawkeye and Thich Nhat Hanh, both mindful speakers and leaders in meditation and mindfulness. I was beginning to truly understand it.

True mindfulness can help us become more spiritual. Whether indulging in mother nature or finding tranquility in the overall action of life itself. For me, I have a sense that there is something greater out there than me as a human being. Whether it be the spirit of a loving and mindful being, mother nature, or something else, I find myself a spiritual person.

I took martial arts classes in my youth. I took Shaolin Kempo, Tai Chi, and Chi Gong. In Tai Chi, we learned meditation is still form as well as meditation in movement. We did it outside, on hills, in the water, balancing on logs, and in the inclement weather. It was truly peaceful and would ground me in the moment and make my day better afterwards. Some people can find peace in meditation. You can learn breathing techniques that can help ground you in your moments of anger, sadness, hopelessness, anxiousness, helplessness, and confusion. If you have racing thoughts and need to calm down, this can help with those as well.

There are many books that can teach you the basic fundamentals of being mindful and you can also go as far as to enroll in a Tai Chi or Chi Gong class for mindful body practices. But if that's not your cup of tea, or you don't have the time or money to attend these classes, you can easily learn about mindfulness and begin to practice it in your everyday activities.

I spent almost 40 days in my intensive inpatient therapy for mental health. When I went in, I was scared and didn't know what to expect. Like anyone else I wanted to go home, but I knew that I was not healthy enough to go home. After learning coping skills and ways to overcome the many obstacles in life, I felt like I was prepared to face anything. The hardest part was going home and putting all those skills to work. The hardest part was also going right back into the same environment that you left, that very well put you in therapy in the first place.

When I was told I was getting discharged in a few days, it hit me. It hit me that being in the program was the easiest thing for me. I was in a safe place, learning the tools to cope with my feelings and that no major stress was being put on my shoulders. It hit me. It hit me that the hardest thing now was going home. Going home, going back to the job and learning to focus on me. Me, myself and I. Loving me. Spoiling me. Selfish me. Me.

I started to feel anxious, and slightly depressed knowing that I was leaving such an amazing place, atmosphere, and people. I started to realize that I needed to ground myself and not let my emotions affect me the same way they did before I went into treatment. I grabbed a guitar, found a quiet spot, laid down looking at the sky, and began to just play. The sound was beautiful and echoed across the field. I was focusing on the beauty of the sound and the dragonflies that seemed to be attracted to the sound of the guitar. I was lost. I was lost in the moment and not a single thing could make me feel sad at that moment.

A smile slowly started to drift over my face. My eyes lightened up, and my breath became slower and more invisible. I felt nothing physically. The fingers on my left hand felt no strings, and my thumb and index finger on my right hand felt no pick. My back felt no pain as I laid on the concrete edge of a resting area, and I was completely lost in the moment. It was the first time that I truly was experiencing mindfulness. I was in a tranquil moment of nothing but positive feelings. It was an experience I wish I could just hand out in jars.

Before I left the facility I was in, I shared a few words with the residents that were there. Some would be leaving soon, and some had just got there, but I wanted them to think about something. I said,

"Live each day here like you're going home tomorrow. You will feel like you're not ready, but as a result, you will be even more eager to learn as much as you can to better prepare you for the journey back to the environment that brought you here."

Do yourself a favor and learn about mindfulness. I can promise you that once you discover it, it will change your world. You will realize that things are not so bad. And look, you don't have to be playing a guitar in a quiet area. You can be walking, brushing your teeth, doing the dishes, eating your favorite food, or even go as far as to be one in nature. I find true tranquility in nature. But just remember, mindfulness is being in the moment for that moment only. Nothing matters but that moment and the positive effect on you for that moment. Live for the moment, in spirituality or within your deity. Your tranquility is key.

The note I wrote on the entrance dry erase board the day I left.

Chapter 10

Reintroduction, Renewal, and Success

Most of the things that I have written in this book will be covered again in this chapter. The reason being is if you are like me at all, you may have forgot the important shit already. I will urge you to re-read chapter 8 again and again until you get the basic steps under your belt. I wouldn't have put them in here if I didn't think they would be important, and believe me they are.

You were once a happier person. You had the desire to do great things and be a great person. You aspired to be a great firefighter or first responder and perhaps a leader as well. You wanted to be the best husband, wife, partner, friend, brother, or sister that you could be. You wanted to be great. We all want to be great.

Someone once told me that firefighters are trained to deal with trauma and horrible things. That is the biggest lie I have ever heard. No one can be trained to wipe out the horrible things they see. From some of the most senior firemen in our past to today, each scene affects us differently.

Detroit Firefighter Dave Parnell said it best in his world-famous quote;

"I wish my head could forgetwhat my eyes have seen."

These words bore truth, hurt, and yet understanding. Understanding from those of us that can relate to that quote. Why else would it be one of the most famous words spoken in the fire service as it relates to mental health?

We are ordinary people who take on unordinary things. We see the strangest things, the most horrific things, and yet the most amazing things too. Just as amazing things never leave our mind because somewhere, they have impacted our heart, the most horrible scenes never leave our mind because of how they have impacted our heart as well. Our heart takes on so much hurt because we don't nurture it, and the same goes with our mind.

Our mind stores memories and emotions in our amygdala as well as survival instincts. We can go back to the fight-or-flight mode and this directly correlates with that. When our sympathetic nervous system gets triggered by something such as fear, we get an adrenaline dump causing our heart to race, blood pressure to rise, and our breathing to increase. This happens on extremely stressful runs because we all fear what? We fear the worst outcomes. Psychologists call this the amygdala hijack.

Back in the caveman times, the amygdala stored the emotion of fear to protect them against the threat of the preying animals of that time. As we evolved as humans, so did the ability to detect threats. We know that if we are faced with a bear or large animal, we may die as the result of injury. This was taught to us in our childhood by our parents, or those who raised us.

My father yelled at me and instilled fear into me as a child. He put his hands around my neck, instilling fear in me as a child. As I got older, anytime someone would yell at me in anger or touch my throat, it triggered fear, hurt, helplessness, and guilt. As a result, the adrenaline would dump, and my heart would race. As we have evolved, many things have been instilled in us that activate the amygdala, and some things that literally are not physically dangerous to us!

The more and more the activation, the more and more the body compensates just to try and operate on a baseline level. We become stressed, our mind becomes convoluted, nothing is working right, you can't get your thoughts under control, and things are starting to bother you in ways that they never did before. As I have listed before, then comes the physical health problems along with the mental health problems. And because of the physical and physiological health problems, that makes you have even more mental health problems. It's a never-ending circle of a long and horrible death. A miserable one at that.

Look, I am not here to blow sunshine up your ass. I'm not. I'm here to tell you that even though I don't know you, or know your struggles directly, I know that you have a good heart and want to be a good person, otherwise you wouldn't be reading this book. But look at this, you are good person, you just lost your way and just need those directions back to the right location.

This all depends on you. No one is going to do this for you. No one can fix you. No one has the miracle to snap their fingers and make you feel whole again. No one can teach you mindfulness, but they can teach you ways to find it. No one can teach you how to forget what your eyes have seen, but they can teach you how to cope with it. No one can hold your hand and guide you through the entire process. You need to swallow your pride and walk the line.

The process is not easy. If it was, no one would ever have mental health problems. And, on top of that, mental health problems do not make you any less of a person. Not at all. Yeah, I'm just another firefighter saying this to you, but I have been there. I had to swallow my pride. I had to cut ties with negativity because she is such a bitch and always brings me down. I had to build my new temple, but my temple must be cleaned every single day. I cannot allow my temple to get vines, mold, or bugs. I must maintain it in the same way I would have to maintain the tools that I use on my job.

I was told before I went into the program, that when I finish I may be a completely different person. In a way I was, but in a way I wasn't. I learned tools to cope with the things that changed me as a person in a negative way. I didn't change as a person. I am still the caring, loving, and intelligent person that I was years ago, it's just that now I will be more caring and loving toward myself.

Getting out was different for a few days. I had learned new coping skills to maintain my anxiety and control my outbursts. Like I said in the quote that I wrote on the dry erase board, you are going back into the environment that brought you to crisis. You're being reintroduced to the lion's den but you have the tools to calm the lions. You have the tools to nurture, care, and respect them that way they can do the same to you.

I have been faced with tests since my release. Some tests that really hit me and brought me to the door of a bad place, but I had the tools to control that bad place and turn it into a victorious win. It is a matter of taking a moment to breathe and ask yourself if you will gain anything positive out of how you handle the situation.

I enjoy firearms. I have several that I have collected and some that I have built. I have never wished to cause harm to a single person with it, and I truly hope I never have to protect myself in fear of taking someone's life to save my own. However, when I came back home after treatment I began to reintroduce firearms into my life. I had a very emotional moment as I gripped the same pistol that I almost took my own life with. It was a scary moment for me, almost to the point that I feared it.

To overcome this feeling, and many other feelings of fear, you must relearn to respect it. Know that things you fear have reasons that you fear them. If it's something that could kill you, make you sad or very unhappy. Understand and respect those facts, but don't let them deter you from being you and from being happy. Don't let your fear for something control who you are. Respect it, and grow with it.

In the case of my firearms, it is going to the range again and practicing trigger discipline, shooting and control of the weapon. It is almost like learning all over again. It is knowing that this is a tool for me, but a tool that could hurt me and someone else if I am not appropriately acquainted with it. The thought of that set my mind at ease and made the transition easier.

This all will be an everyday thing for the rest of your life, but the more you continue to learn, the more you practice your skills, and the more you believe in yourself, the easier it will be to transition back into a healthy life. It will eventually get to the point that you don't realize that you're even doing it. It's like muscle memory, but it's just you, being awesome and you loving yourself. You need to love yourself, that's key. Only you can love yourself. In the words of RuPaul,

"If you don't love yourself, how the hell you gonna love somebody else."

Do yourself this favor. Look at yourself in the mirror. Look closely. Don't say a single thing, just look at it and focus on it. Look at the reflection in the mirror. Look at your eyebrows, the color of your hair, the tone of your skin and texture. The shape of your chin, the corner of your mouth and the color of your eyes. Pay attention to every small detail you can and make it a point to think about each thing you look at. Don't focus on anything else but. Don't think, "Oh man, I am breaking out", or anything like that. Just look at it. What do you see? Really, what do you see? Do you see tired eyes? Do you see wrinkles? Look at it. That image is you. That image on the outside will change in time, but regardless of the features, someone will always be able to recognize you.

Now smile. Look at your smile. Can you make it look genuine, or does it look fake? Seriously, think of something now that can make you smile, and while you smile look at it. That is what you need to strive for more often, and I know you can do it. The outside is always different than the inside. If one positive thought can make you smile, then a million positive thoughts can make you smile. And while we live for the moment, not for the day, we can think one happy thought to make us smile, every moment, of every day, and that's 960 moments. Make 960 memories that bring you a smile and add an extra 960 for reserve. When you run out of positive memories to fill those moments, make it a goal to make more, and more, and more.

This is all on you my brother, my sister. This is all on you. All I can do is support your decision to become the person you want to become. There are a lot of people that want you to become the best person you can become. Look for those people in your life, because if they are not for you, then they need to leave the picture, and you need to make the room for the other person who is for you. Success depends on you.

The Guiding Light

When times were rough, I was lost at best.
My mind so cluttered I could not rest.
There were answers out there that I never knew.
But the guiding light sent me to you.
The wind gusts strong, the mountains high.
My legs too weak for me to climb.
I once was strong but so confused.
Till the guiding light sent me to you.
My soul felt empty, the trunk now hollow.
The trail too hard for me to follow.
I felt so lost, through and through.
So the guiding light sent me to you.
Your hands now open, I walk inside.
I take a breath, swallow my pride.
Time to make the moments true.
Because the guiding light sent me to you.
At times my clock could not tell time.
I'd think that it was my final sign.
But the battery has now been renewed.
Because the guiding light sent me to you.
No waves too high to make life grim.
You've given me courage to take the swim.
A journey ahead, my life anew.
Thanks to the light that sent me to you.
-Melissa Parker-
08-29-2019

Resources for First Responders

IAFF Center of Excellence For Behavioral Health Treatment and Recovery

844-709-9345

http://www.iaffrecoverycenter.com

National Volunteer Fire Council

888-731-3473

http://www.nvfc.org

Code Green Campaign

206-459-3020

http://www.codegreencampaign.org

American Addiction Centers

888-557-8224

http://www.americanaddictioncenters.org

Vermont Center for Responder Wellness

802-661-4376

https://vtresponderwellness.com

Warriors' Ascent

816-800-9276

https://www.warriorsascent.org

Kill 22 Outreach Program

214-462-7229

http://www.22kill.com